C000130687

Planely Schmitz

Planely Schmitz

Sebastian Schmitz

ISBN 978-0-9932604-1-4

© 2016 Astral Horizon Aviation Press. All rights reserved.

79 Wardour Street London W1D 6QB United Kingdom

www.theairlineboutique.com

PLANELY SCHMITZ

An Airline Anthology

Sebastian Schmitz

It's all Charlie's fault. Charles Kennedy is a very special friend of mine, fellow writer for various aviation magazines, pilot, music legend and I don't know what else. He was the one who ultimately convinced me that it would be a nice idea to compile a 'Best of' (with a bit of 'Making of') bringing together some of the articles I have written and which have appeared (verbatim or in a very similar version) in aviation magazines around the world over the last fifteen years. All of the articles featured here are unique in their own way and I hope the comments below them reveal why. Flying is pure magic to me (except going in a fully booked A321 to Tenerife) and I am sure it will never cease to be. I have spent some of the happiest moments of my life in aeroplanes. Writing articles has also often been a reason or justification to go to a place I'd otherwise not have visited. I hope you enjoy reading these articles, even though you may have seen them before. Others never made it into the magazines and are published here for the first time. Enjoy this book. Thanks, Charlie!

Hemus Air

(appeared in Air International May 2001)

Whilst not particularly well known outside Bulgaria, Hemus Air is now the second-largest airline in the country and, since the privatisation of Balkan, is due to become the national carrier. With its current fleet of Russian- and Czech-built aircraft, Hemus is serving a growing network of destinations all over Europe and the Middle East on both scheduled and charter flights.

Named after the Balkan mountain range (which is 'Hemus' in Latin), Hemus Air was formed on November 20, 1991, having previously operated a handful of Mil Mi-8s on special contracts as the helicopter division of Balkan Airlines. It was launched as a separate airline when Bulgaria's Ministry of Aviation decreed that some Balkan Airlines flights should be operated by an independent airline. The destinations under consideration were the thinner routes in the Balkan region.

At its inauguration, the Hemus fleet consisted of three Yakovlev Yak-40s and two Tupolev Tu-134s. However, it was soon realised that the airline had too many aircraft for too few flights; indeed, the only route served in 1991 was Sofia to the Albanian capital of Tirana. Consequently the management looked towards the charter business and this remains a major source of income for Hemus Air today. The three Yak-40s were leased to Nigeria on a long-term contract and the Tu-134s were used for the scheduled services to Tirana, as well as a number of charters throughout Europe. It was not long before a second destination was introduced: Skopje, the capital of the now-independent former Yugoslav republic of Macedonia, only a short hop from Sofia. Both Tirana and Skopje still form part of the network.

Hemus Air was able to branch out from its regional status in late 1991, when Balkan gave up its route to Oslo. Hemus jumped in — a move which has come to exemplify the company's route policy. Whenever Balkan abandons a route, Hemus is keen to adopt it. The same thing happened recently when Balkan was denied traffic rights to both the Lebanon and Syria, because Israeli investors had bought a major stake in the company. This provided the perfect opportunity for Hemus Air to expand once again. Almost immediately, Tu-134s began flying to Beirut twice a week. The Syrian capital, Damascus, is now number one on the airline's shopping list — negotiations with the Syrian authorities are underway and by the time this article is published, Damascus may have become the latest addition to the Hemus network.

Meanwhile, back at the beginning; after flights began to Oslo, a combined service was launched in 1992 to Leipzig (Germany) via Bratislava (Slovakia). With a much lower cost structure and aircraft better suited to thinner routes, Hemus Air can get better returns than Balkan. Prior to 2000, the two carriers had never flown as direct competitors, but that changed last spring when Hemus Air offered up to three daily flights between Sofia and Varna. Hemus has a clear advantage over Balkan's Antonov An-24 turboprops, as it offers an all-jet service with Yak-40s and, when the demand is higher, Tu-134s; furthermore it has an in-flight service which provides a cold meal. Another route flown in competition with Balkan is the domestic run to Bourgas, which is served daily during the summer using Yak-40s and the airline's single Let-410.

June 2000 brought the introduction of a new — and so far, biggest — aircraft to join the fleet. Tupolev Tu-154M LZ-HMP was leased from Gyandzha-based Turan Air of Azerbaijan, to be operated on holiday charters out of the Black Sea resorts of Varna and Bourgas to destinations such as Berlin and Dresden in Germany, Billund and Copenhagen in Denmark, Krakow and Katowice in Poland, as well as Dubai (United Arab Emirates) and Doha (Qatar) in the Persian Gulf. With the acquisition of the 152-seat aircraft, Hemus Air hopes to join Air Via and Balkan in the profitable holiday business. Such was the demand for the Tu-154 that the company has recently acquired a second example (LZ-HMS) in time for the 2001 summer season.

With regards to expansion, Hemus Air has always pursued a 'one step at a time' policy, as Managing Director Dimitar Pavlov explained: "This strategy of controlled growth instead of rapid expansion has brought us to where we stand today. Hence there is no need to change our policy." It is most likely that this combination of slow but continuous growth and a commitment to various business sectors is what has made Hemus Air successful, despite the severe economic problems that Bulgaria is facing today. It is these economic considerations, as well as political developments in the Balkan region, that will be the main factors affecting the airline's future expansion.

Another hurdle will be privatisation. While most state-owned companies, such as Balkan and the various airports, have been sold to private investors, Hemus Air remains one hundred percent state-owned. A proposal to privatise the airline in mid-January was delayed after the Privatisation Agency extended the deadline for submitting formal bids for a fifty-one percent stake until February 12. The latest bid extension is the third time the government has deferred the privatisation process since it first announced its intent reduce its shareholding back in the third quarter of 1999.

There are still more plans afoot — the acquisition of western-built aircraft is the second most important point on the agenda, with Boeing 737s and BAe 146s being considered for 2001. Indeed, it would appear that Hemus does not have much choice. It is becoming more difficult (i.e. expensive) to fly the Tu-134 into noise-sensitive Western European airports. In addition, the Russian aircraft are rather thirsty — and current high oil prices are another reason to look for a replacement. For the time being, Hemus seems to have found a good compromise with the Tu-154M. Certainly the jump from a Tu-134 to a Tu-154 is much easier for the flight crews than it would be if they were converting onto western aircraft. Furthermore, the Tu-154s are robust and, equally importantly, certified under Stage III noise regulations, considerably reducing landing fees. However, while management is seriously seeking alternatives for the Russian jets, the director of Hemus Air's maintenance facilities is of a different opinion: "There is still life in the Tupolevs — they are easy to maintain and are paid off. There is no need to buy anything else."

The company is particularly proud of its maintenance facilities, which can undertake all airframe repairs. Its work even meets the strict requirements of the German aviation authorities — Director Pavlov explained that its Yak-40s on scheduled flights out of Leipzig were regularly being delayed by the German authorities as they carried out ramp checks, so Hemus Air responded by inviting the Germans to Sofia to inspect its maintenance facilities and procedures. There have not been ramp checks since.

Hemus Air has formed interline agreements with several European carriers, though there are no immediate plans to codeshare. Several aircraft are leased to Albanian Airlines, the Albanian flag carrier, on a long-term contract, including Tu-134s and Yak-40s, depending upon demand. The aircraft are wet-leased (with crews) and all maintenance work — except for minor line checks — is carried out in Sofia. Another Yak-40, LZ-DOM, is currently on lease to another Albanian airline, ADA Air. Long-term contracts, such as those with the two Albanian carriers, have certainly helped the carrier survive rough periods. Hemus Air is also keen to capitalise on the as-yet-underdeveloped executive market and for this purpose it operates a Yak-40 (LZ-DOS) equipped with a 16-seat VIP interior. Customers include politicians and various important or wealthy (or both) private clients. Even famous rock stars have made use of the sofa and TV-equipped LZ-DOS.

Last but not least, Hemus Air operates a Yak-40 for calibration duties on behalf of the Bulgarian aviation authorities. Registered LZ-DOE, it is the only Yak-40 still sporting the airline's former — and rather attractive — colour scheme. With regard to the new corporate identity, the maintenance director explains that "white looks beautiful and modern". If flight safety ranks first on the airline's list of priorities, in-flight service occupies second place. Meals are served on all flights, even on short hops from Sofia to Skopje or Varna.

Although Hemus Air serves only a limited number of destinations, it does offer connections through Sofia. Passengers from Oslo can continue their journey to Skopje or Tirana (and many do), whilst those from Leipzig can change aircraft in Sofia for onwards travel to the Middle East. The airline's tiny head office, located in a garden next to the airport, may look rather modest and basic, but it has proved perfectly suited to Hemus Air's needs. The employees, both in administration and on board the aircraft, are courteous and their manner pleasant. It is hoped that the company's positive spirit survives an uncertain future.

This was my first ever article published in an English-language aviation magazine. It happened purely by coincidence. At the time, I was one of two guys running Airevents, a small company chartering mostly Russian aircraft for enthusiast sightseeing flights. We tried to charter aircraft during their transit times and to convince airlines this was a nice extra business for them and good promotion of their scheduled services. It was mostly smaller airlines that became interested and Hemus Air was one of them. They operated scheduled flights from Sofia to Leipzig via Bratislava (full traffic rights on all sectors) with their Yak-40s. Can you imagine that in 2015! And they were happy to charter out a Yak-40 for sightseeing flights out of Leipzig on several occasions. The station manager of Hemus Air in Leipzig, Mrs Prangova, was very enthusiastic about these flights and when I suggested I could write an article about the airline for a magazine (something I had never done before), it took her a heartbeat to love the idea and invite me to Sofia.

Hemus Air is still around today, although not under that name. Hemus purchased the successor of Balkan, Bulgaria Air, in 2006. Operations were merged under the more catchy 'Bulgaria Air' brand and some of Hemus Air's aircraft became the dowry in this Bulgarian airline marriage. Most of Hemus Air's Russian-built fleet were deemed no longer useful and some still remain in storage at Sofia Airport today, a quiet reminder of this fine little airline. When the article about Hemus Air was published in Air International, I was so proud to read my name under something printed, I knew I wanted to continue writing articles in some form or the other. And here we are, fifteen years later...

Easter Island Airport
(published in Airports Of The World September / October 2013)

Easter Island ('Isla de Pascua' in Spanish) is the world's most remote inhabited island, located about halfway between Chile (the closest point in Chile is 2,191 miles or 3,526 kilometers to the east) and Tahiti in the Pacific Ocean (2,641 miles / 4,251 kilometers to the west). Most famous for its mysterious stone statues, the Moai, the island is increasingly becoming a tourist destination. The island is called Easter Island because it was discovered by Dutchman Jakob Roggeveen on Easter Sunday 1722. Being so far away from the rest of the world, Easter Island's Mataveri International Airport plays a key role in developing the island's tourism. All visitors to the island, except for the occasional cruise ship passengers, arrive on the island by plane. And so does every other item you can imagine, from food to spare parts or even toilet paper.

Mataveri Airport (IATA code: IPC / ICAO code: SCIP) is the world's most remote commercial airport. It is located in the island's south, with the long runway literally cutting through the island from one coast to the other. It is just a short walk away from the only town on the island, Hanga Roa. The airport has been the island's aerial gateway since 1967, when the first commercial aircraft, a LAN DC-6, landed at the newly-built facility. The actual first flight to Easter Island had already taken place much earlier, in 1951, carried out by a PBY-6A Catalina that landed on what was only a provisional runway. One year after the first commercial flight by LAN, in 1968, the route from Santiago to Easter Island was extended to Tahiti. In 1970, the DC-6 was replaced by more modern Boeing 707s and in April 2012, LAN celebrated 45 years of continuous service to the island. When the airport opened, it not only made Easter Island much more accessible but also opened the door to transpacific flying, as there was now a suitable diversion airport en route between Australia and Oceania and South America.

There is only one airline serving Mataveri airport with scheduled flights: Chilean carrier LAN. The number of flights to their homebase Santiago de Chile has increased significantly during the last years. Some years ago, depending on the season, LAN operated only two weekly flights, a number that increased during high season. Today, throughout most of the year, there is at least one daily flight between Easter Island and Santiago, sometimes even two. The flight time from Santiago is between four-and-a-half and five hours, almost entirely over water. LAN's flights arrive at Easter Island from Santiago around lunchtime, returning about an hour later. Once a week, the flight from Santiago continues on to Tahiti. This route is quite popular with around-the-world-travellers on their way from South America to the Pacific region.

In addition to that, although Easter Island belongs to Chile, the island is culturally closer to Polynesia and links are quite strong, with people frequently travelling back and forth. In January 2011, in addition to its flights to Santiago and Tahiti, LAN launched a flight between Lima in Peru and Easter Island for the first time. It was flown twice a week in a triangular Lima-Easter Island-Santiago routing or vice versa. This route was aiming at tourists wishing to combine a visit to the many sights in Peru with Easter Island more easily, without having to go via Santiago. In the next two peak season periods, January-March 2012 and 2013, the route was relaunched for a few weeks but halted prematurely both years and passengers rebooked on services via Santiago, as passenger numbers stayed below the airline's expectations. As of early 2013, it is uncertain whether flights to Lima will be revived for the high season next year. All of LAN's flights to Easter Island are flown by Boeing 767-300s, an aircraft perfectly suited for the long overwater flight and with sufficient capacity to carry the large amounts of cargo that are usually carried to Easter Island.

Apart from LAN's scheduled flights, no other airlines serve Easter Island on a regular basis and commercial visitors are rather rare. Being such a remote and exotic place, halfway between South America and Oceania, Easter Island is often a stop on luxurious around-the-world itineraries. During his visit to the airport, the author was lucky enough to witness the visit of a Thomson Boeing 757 chartered by TCS Starquest Expeditions for an around-the-world expedition. The aircraft stayed on the ground for two days, arriving from Peru and departing for Samoa. Such a visit is representative of the luxury charter sector and airlines that have landed here include QANTAS, Icelandair,

Travel Service, First Choice and Air New Zealand. In 2012, the airport recorded a total of 168,485 passengers. The largest share travelled to and from Santiago, 135,081; the remaining 33,404 to and from Lima and Papeete. Traffic has grown rapidly as frequencies are added (to illustrate the point, in 2003 Mataveri Airport only recorded 49,816 travellers).

On the cargo side, 4,066 tons of cargo were transhipped at the airport's small cargo terminal, just next to the passenger terminal. With most every supply arriving at the island by air, the shares of incoming and outgoing cargo are very uneven, with very little cargo leaving and much more arriving.

Because of its remote location and the nearest diversion airport more than four hours away, there are some quite unique rules for aircraft operating to Easter Island. Before reaching the so-called Equal Time Point (the geographical point in a flight where the distance to the destination is the same as the distance back to the origin), aircraft have to obtain the latest weather data. No other aircraft en route to Easter Island can depart before the preceding flight has passed its Equal Time Point. Before reaching its Equal Time Point, the second aircraft must ensure that the preceding flight has landed on Easter Island safely and cleared the runway. (A parallel runway which could be used as a backup runway in an emergency would ease these operational constraints significantly.) Refuelling is possible on the island — there is a fuel farm close to the airport housing not only Jet A-1 for the aircraft but also the fuel for cars driving on the island. Fuel is brought in by ship from the mainland every few weeks.

The airport's name Mataveri means 'beautiful eyes' in the islanders' local language Rapa Nui. Yet the terminal of Mataveri Airport is not so beautiful for the eyes, as it has seen better days and is not really up to modern standards. The main check-in hall is reminiscent of a parking garage, lit by neon lights and not very inviting. There is one central LAN check-in at the far end of the building, with the rest of the space occupied by some shops, mostly selling Easter Island memorabilia and tourist kitsch. Through a small corridor, departing passengers can pass through security (and passport control when they fly to Lima or Tahiti) and enter the waiting hall, some of which is open-air. Here once more, the building is not particularly nice and also not taken care of in the manner one would hope for at a destination as Easter Island, where nearly all visitors come and go by plane.

Plans for a total overhaul and upgrade of the airport do exist, the core project being a new, more sophisticated passenger terminal designed in the typical architecture of the island. The new terminal building, together with an expanded apron, will be able to handle up to four large aircraft at a time, where now the maximum is two. The airport's single runway 10 / 28, measuring 10,827 x 148 feet (3,300 x 45 meters), will receive a parallel taxiway, which will also serve as a secondary runway, for example when the main runway cannot be used because of an accident or is under repair. For now the small apron is linked to the runway by two short taxiways and aircraft have to backtrack the runway after landing or before take-off.

Taking a picture of a LAN Boeing 767 is a lot easier at a number of different airports in South or North America and even the most extreme enthusiast would probably not travel to Easter Island to go plane spotting. If, however, one is on the island for all the other good reasons to go there, a dash of aviation photography can be done quite easily. There are a few nice vantage points around the airport — a road surrounds the entire airport and one can simply follow it to explore the perimeter. The airport is surrounded by a fence which is too tightly meshed to allow decent pictures.

Most interesting for taking pictures is the eastern end of the airport, near the threshold of runway 28. Here, the road is quite a bit higher than the runway and from this elevated position, pictures of aircraft on the runway can be taken with ease. The area around the terminal and along the western end of the runway is nice for viewing but, because of the fence, not really ideal for taking pictures. Those with an enormous telephoto lens might want to explore one of the nearby hills as a vantage point. When arriving or departing, nice pictures of the aircraft can be taken easily, either when walking to or from the aircraft or from the boarding area. Because many of the passengers are taking pictures when boarding or de-boarding, airport staff are used to this.

Easter Island is not only one of the world's most remote but also one of the most spectacular places, even when it´s only for admiring the mystical stone statues, the Moai, that are dotted all around the island. A visit here will definitely be a most rewarding experience for any visitor and, with modernisation under way, Mataveri International Airport will hopefully soon be an equally lovely gateway to the island.

In terms of remoteness, it doesn't get much better than Easter Island. When you watch the airshow onboard the plane, you see nothing but water and one little dot — that's Easter Island. It was somewhere I have always wanted to visit, simply because it is so far away from anything else and because I always found the mystical statues ('Moai') on the island somewhat intriguing. Was it nice there? Definitely. Was it magical? Not really, well maybe the tuna and cheese empanadas that they sold on the island's only real beach. Other than that, it was quite okay to spend a few days there but I wouldn't rush back to Easter Island again. The article about the airport was a by-product of a holiday as many airport articles are (which is not meant to belittle them). When one travels to exotic places to take pictures at the airport, sometimes you realise that there is actually enough material for a nice article. That's what happens to me sometimes and I guess it happens to other aviation writers, too.

By Ilyushin Il-18 to Mogadishu

(appeared in Airways September 2007)

After years of civil war, Mogadishu, the capital of Somalia, is not in the best shape, with the country itself divided and in anarchic chaos, administered by clan chiefs or anybody with enough money (read: weapons). Recently, neighbouring Ethiopia became involved in military actions, including the bombing of Mogadishu Airport. Somaliland, the northern part of Somalia, has declared itself independent, although this has not been acknowledged internationally. Over many years of travel, it has been my experience that often the most bizarre destinations have proved to be harmless or surprisingly pleasant and civilised. However, the main reason for my visit to Mogadishu was neither country nor city, as I intended to spend only two hours there. The means of travel held the most attraction: a Daallo Airlines Ilyushin Il-18.

The adventure starts with a wake-up call in Dubai at 02:00 in the morning, for a flight on a Kyrgyzstan-registered Daallo Boeing 737 to Djibouti. Check-in at Dubai International is open when I arrive, but the queues are a bit confusing, resembling a meandering river delta. However, the process is quite efficient, and soon afterward I head toward the departure gate. I discover that although the gate is open, there is not the slightest indication of when boarding might actually start. Suddenly a fight starts when a woman dressed in white attacks a man in a suit, shouting and screaming at him. Some fellow passengers tell me that she had apparently been promised a new life in Europe — evidently the man was somehow involved in the 'arrangement' — and paid lots of money for the opportunity. But the new life ended in Dubai and she is on her way back home.

The passengers are mostly Somalians, and some of them seem to be real VIPs. A traveller sitting next to me in the waiting lounge says: "Look, the man over there is the biggest clan chief in Mogadishu, he has many, many firearms and guns." That revelation does nothing to put my mind at rest. Later, onboard, another passenger would not allow the flight attendant to stow his case in the overhead bin, as it is "full of money." Another fight erupts onboard between two hotheads over where one should, and should not, stow his luggage.

To my relief, we are finally airborne. My seat in business class (one of eight, the remainder economy) is excellent, with very good seat pitch. Cabin service is fine too, with the best scrambled eggs I have ever had on an airplane (author's note from 2015: this statement is still valid, things didn't get better). I even manage to fit in two hours of sleep before landing in Djibouti.

Djibouti's Ambouli airport is dominated by military activity. Traditionally, the French Air Force maintains a large force here and the German Navy stations some aircraft at this strategically important airport. Transit time is a little over an hour and the process quite smooth. Passengers are brought to the small terminal building by bus, then given a transit boarding pass and told to wait in the lounge. After about half an hour, we are taken to the Il-18. Djibouti is in one of the hottest regions in the world, and this is amply demonstrated as we enter the airplane: the Il-18 does not have air conditioning, at least not on the ground. About eighty passengers take their seats and are greeted by the half-Kyrgyz, half-Somali crew (the airplane belongs to Phoenix Aviation, based in Kyrgyzstan).

The flight to Mogadishu usually routes via Hargeisa, but this airport is undergoing maintenance so today, we will land at Berbera, in Somaliland (the would-be independent part of Somalia). Sector time is only about thirty-five minutes, and the air conditioning starts to work shortly after takeoff. We also receive very welcome refreshment towels and drinks. Berbera supposedly has one of the longest runways in Africa, extended by the Soviets as a landing site for their space shuttle Buran, but only a very small terminal and no fences. Everybody seems to be running about the place without any control whatsoever. Most of the eighty passengers deplane here, while those destined for Mogadishu go for a walk in the furnace-like heat.

At departure time, sixteen passengers are onboard for Mogadishu, as a thorough head count by the flight attendant reveals. I am fortunate to ride in the cockpit, along with the four-man crew, for the descent into Mogadishu. The closer we approach, the more I start wondering where the airport is. Even when we land on a very small gravel strip, a terminal building is not readily apparent. Mogadishu's international airport has been closed for some time, after a brief re-opening was ended by Ethiopian attacks. Previously, it had been closed for years because of conflicts over ownership between different clans. A replacement has been found in "Kilometre No. 50 Airport", shorthand "Kilometre Fifty" or "Mogadishu Fifty", so-named because of its distance south of the city, although the terminal is small and lacks much in the way of infrastructure. I search in vain for the duty free shop, then check-in for the return flight after being shown around by a representative of Daallo. After an hour or so our flight is ready to depart.

When in Mogadishu, would you be worried by the sight of a mechanic climbing up a ladder to attend to a problem with your airplane? I do not relish the thought of an overnight here. Everybody else seems quite relaxed however, so I decide to take it easy and walk around the apron, terminal, and the surrounding 'landside' area. Some farmers with goats cross the runway. Meanwhile, the mechanics and all members of the Il-18's cockpit crew work on the number three Ivchenko AI-20 turbine.

A generator has to be replaced, but fortunately they have all the spare parts onboard — and, in their heads, the knowledge to carry out the repair. At least I hope they do. Most of the passengers for the return flight have taken their seats — in the shade beneath the aircraft's wings, by far the best place to be. Those who have already boarded the aircraft soon regret the move, because the temperature inside the cabin is constantly rising. The boarding stairs need to be moved around to give the mechanics better access to the engine, so for about an hour nobody is able to go onboard or deplane.

I chat with the flight engineer (whose mouth is replete with gold teeth), an Indian passenger who has a business in Mogadishu, a Somali boy who speaks Russian (he learnt it from the flight engineer during many visits to Mogadishu), and others. Another little boy, who proves to be very innovative, sets up a business — a sort of mobile duty free shop — specialising in mussels from the nearby coast. The stewardess buys some. By now the cabin is a sauna. But to almost every problem there is a solution: the passengers stuck inside simply remove the emergency window exits to breathe fresh air.

Some time later we are invited to board. But there is still a problem. The ground handling people evidently do not deem it necessary to bring the aircraft stairs back around to the passenger entry door. Again there is a 'creative' solution: boarding by ladder. (The women, especially, do not appreciate this inconvenience.)

On the flight to Berbera a hot dinner is served: rice with something with the consistency and taste of shoe soles, and french fries. Transit time at Berbera is a little over an hour, allowing for a pleasant walk around the ramp. Two Saudis board the airplane with falcons perched on their shoulders. Upon entering the rear cabin they are met with protests from most of the passengers. But an Indian passenger stoically says, "No problem" when one of the falconers sits down beside him. Immediately, the bird defecates on his trousers, leaving a strong smell and strange colour, yet the Indian remains surprisingly calm. The falcons appear the most relaxed about the situation; indeed, they seem to be quite seasoned flyers — without even having to flap their wings for propulsion. Perhaps they are grateful for someone else to do the heavy lifting, for a change.

After some rushed seat changes due to falconophobia (I just invented that word), we depart on the last leg to Djibouti. The Russian flight attendant becomes angry because there is hardly any water left for the passengers, but only seconds later she smiles brightly when a passenger hands her a bottle of perfume as a gift. An exciting day comes to an end as the sun sets, and I enjoy a glass of beer at the airport bar before the return flight by 737-200 to Dubai. I sleep for the entire three hours and only wake up when we touch down.

The flight I took is probably the best — if not the only — way to sample an Il-18 these days, and I can highly recommend the experience. However, all sensible precautions should be taken and warnings heeded seriously. A stay in Somalia is not recommended. In February, for example, a gun battle took place close to the Kilometre Fifty airstrip, and in March Ugandan troops arriving at the newly opened Mogadishu International Airport were greeted by mortar rounds. The same month, an Ilyushin Il-76 was shot down after taking off from Mogadishu. Somaliland itself may be considered safe. Bookings may be made through any Daallo Airlines office or at some travel agencies.

The trip down to Mogadishu was among my top three best flights and most exciting trips ever. It was part of an epic two-week journey that encompassed Almaty and Astana in Kazakhstan, where it was freezing cold (it was early January). Kazakhstan was followed by Mogadishu, Amman and a visit to Ramallah in Palestine to visit the grave of Yassir Arafat. From there it was back to Dubai and up to Aleppo in Syria on a flight with Air Arabia before returning to Dubai once more and heading back home from there. Two days after driving through the snow in Almaty in a taxi that smelled like a garlic farm (well, the driver did), I sat on the apron at Mogadishu's improvised Kilometre Fifty airport, protecting myself from the sun under the wings of an Il-18 that had just gone tech. I was somehow hoping that we would get to stay in Mogadishu. That would have been quite a story to tell! At the same time, the coward in me was praying to Allah (or whoever was responsible in that part of the world) that the engineers would be able to fix what was wrong and we could return. We didn't stay and the story of this short visit to Mogadishu is still one of the fondest memories I have when looking through the shelf with my magazines on it. And — Daallo Airlines is still doing business today, in 2015.

First Air — The Arctic Experts
(appeared in Airliner World January 2015)

Challenging weather conditions, very low temperatures, often very basic infrastructure — flying in northern Canada is full of challenges. And yet — for the small communities in the Arctic, it is absolutely essential. First Air, the airline with the most comprehensive network in northern Canada, has been mastering many challenges for almost seventy years now and grown from a small flying school to the leading airline in the region.

Founded by Russell Bradley as Bradley Air Services Limited in 1946, the company was initially a pilot training centre and flying school based in Ottawa. Bradley's innovative spirit and his ability to find profitable niches in which the small company could operate was probably what ensured the company's success in its early years. In the 1950s, Bradley Air Services was awarded a major Geological Survey of Canada contract. It was this important contract that let Bradley and partner Weldy Phipps develop and bring to perfection the large balloon-like 'tundra tires' that allow aircraft like the Twin Otter or smaller types to virtually land anywhere in the High Arctic. Although in 1973 the First Air brand was introduced when scheduled flying started, Bradley Air Services is still the company's legal name. During the first decades of its existence, charter flying and aerial survey work on behalf of scientific institutions and government agencies were the bread and butter of the airline. Operating in the often harsh environment of Canada's far north, First Air and its employees had became true specialists for this part of the world.

Scheduled flying soon became an important pillar in the colourful portfolio of First Air's activities. And while most of its charter work still took place in often very remote parts of Canada, the airline's first scheduled routes in 1973 were somewhat more boring, linking the Canadian capital Ottawa with Sudbury and North Bay in Ontario. Throughout its existence, the company grew both organically and through acquisitions of other carriers or part of them, such as the Baffin Island operations of Survair in 1978, and later Ptarmigan Airways and NWT Air. In 1990, First Air itself was purchased by the Makivik

Corporation, the organisation which represents the Inuit people of northern Quebec, and it remains the airline's owner to this day. While Makivik's principal mandate is the administration of Inuit land, it also operates several businesses in the Nunavik region, including First Air and Air Inuit, a sister company that operates closely with First Air in the Nunavik Region.

In 1986, the first jet aircraft, a Boeing 727-100, joined First Air's colourful fleet, which until then consisted of various single engine aircraft, Twin Otters and the Hawker-Siddeley Hs748 'Budgie' as the biggest aircraft type. As the scheduled network grew, more jets were acquired, both Boeing 727s and the first Boeing 737-200s. These proved to be fantastic value for the airline because of their ability to operate from gravel runways, at least when equipped with the necessary gravel kit. By the turn of the millennium, the first ATR42 turboprops, converted to combi aircraft by First Air's own engineering department, were introduced, more efficient and reliable than the Hs748s. The Budgies were slowly replaced by the ATRs and ultimately retired from service in 2011.

The introduction of a new colour scheme in 2005 consisted of a largely white fuselage topped off with spectacular aircraft tails depicting northern scenes, and today, all aircraft wear a different tail design.

In 2009, First Air acquired its first ever widebody aircraft, a single Boeing 767-200 Freighter, to cope with the ever-growing demand for cargo transportation from southern Canada to the north. In 2011, the ATR72 joined the smaller ATR42s as part of First Air's fleet. Today, First Air has become the largest airline in northern Canada, with thirty-four destinations, around 1,000 employees and operates a fleet of twenty-three aircraft flying on scheduled and charter flights. Apart from its own flying, First Air also provides MRO services to other airlines at its maintenance bases in Ottawa and Yellowknife as well as ground handling services at various airports in Canada.

One thing about First Air's network becomes quite obvious when looking at the airline's route map: it covers a vast area, spanning the Northwest Territories, Nunavut and Nunavik. There are four departure points in southern Canada: Montreal, Ottawa, Winnipeg and Edmonton. These airports are connected to the three northern hubs: Edmonton flights go up to Yellowknife in the NWT, Winnipeg has a route up to Rankin Inlet in Nunavut (the most central point in First Air's network) and Montreal and Ottawa have a route up to the city of Iqaluit (formerly Frobisher Bay), the capital of Nunavut, with Montreal flights also routing through Kuujjuaq, the heart of Nunavik and home of the shareholder of First Air.

The northern hubs offer a plethora of connections in their respective regions and are also connected to each other several times a week by a Yellowknife-Rankin Inlet-Iqaluit return flight. Each of them is an important regional centre, economically, politically and culturally.

Knowing that there are bigger and busier airports in the country such as Toronto, Calgary and Vancouver, one may ask why First Air does not fly to any of them. Well, simply because there is very limited demand. People in the Northwest Territories are very much focussed on Yellowknife as regional centre and Edmonton as 'the big city'. The same applies to the central region, where Rankin Inlet is a regional centre and Winnipeg is where most businesses operating in the area have their base or where people go for medical treatment. For the eastern part of the Canadian Arctic, the regional hubs are Iqaluit and Kuujjuaq, and business, political and cultural links are mostly with Ottawa and Montreal.

Thus, First Air's network is very much suited to everyday demand. Through interline agreements with Air Canada, Westjet and Porter, onward connections to elsewhere in Canada and beyond can still be offered easily. To illustrate the vastness of First Air's network: the flight from Ottawa to Iqaluit takes around three hours, similar to a flight from Ottawa to Miami. The flight from Iqaluit to Resolute Bay, the northernmost destination in First Air's network, is another three hours, at which point one is only halfway across First Air's route map.

One thing that passengers are unlikely to do after a flight with First Air: leave hungry. The airline prides itself in what is probably the best inflight service anywhere in North America. On longer sectors, passengers can expect a free and quite generous hot meal (two breakfast and two dinner options), free beverages (including wine and beer) and delicious fresh-baked cookies. Even on the shortest sectors, there is always a snack and beverage service. The reason why passengers are fed so well? Depending on their destination, this may be the last really nice meal or glass of wine they get for a while (numerous of the communities in Canada's North are 'dry'). The seat pitch of thirty-four inches (on the 737s) is also more than what most carriers in North America offer. What makes First Air very popular with travellers is their extremely generous baggage allowance of two pieces each weighing up to seventy lbs (thirty-two kilograms). When people from the north go to southern Canada, they usually shop a lot and due to the generous baggage allowance are able to bring home what they bought for free.

Through a codeshare agreement with Air Greenland, First Air also offers (seasonal) flights from Iqaluit to Greenland's capital Nuuk, launched in 2012, and are operated by Air Greenland's Dash 8s during the summer months. Until 2001, First Air offered their own flights to Greenland, serving Kangerlussuaq Airport, using Boeing 727 combis.

First Air's fleet, as of autumn 2014, consists of eleven ATR turboprops, nine of which are ATR42s and two bigger ATR72s. All of them have been converted to a combi passenger / cargo aircraft and the version they operate in can be adjusted to demand. The ATRs mostly operate on flights to the northern communities and are not usually seen at First Air's southern airports like Ottawa or Edmonton. The sector length on these flights can be anything from half an hour up to three hours. As a passenger, it is very interesting to travel on the smallest passenger / cargo ratio, with only ten passenger seats installed in a very small cabin in the rear of the ATR42.

First Air's own engineering department, with its main facility at Ottawa airport, performs all maintenance events for the airline. It is one of the few companies in the world holding the ATR42/72 combi conversion Supplemental Type Certificate and offers combi conversions for ATR turboprops to third parties. First Air's team of engineers also recently developed the first-ever nosewheel gravel protection kit for ATR72s. Apart from taking care of First Air's own aircraft, external airline customers have been supplied with maintenance services for decades.

There are six Boeing 737-200s, three of which operate as combi aircraft. The main reason why the Boeing 737-200 is still part of the fleet is because of the ability to land on gravel runways. Some of the airports that First Air operates scheduled flights to, such as Cambridge Bay, have not been upgraded to an asphalt runway (and there are no immediate plans) and some smaller airfields that receive charter flights also only have gravel runways. The ability to offer jet service into those airports has ensured the subtype's survival until this day and as there is no real successor in sight offering the same capabilities, the last Boeing 737-200s will likely remain in First Air's fleet for the coming years, if only to serve gravel runways.

To bring operation costs down and increase passenger comfort, three Boeing 737-400s were added to the fleet in 2013, all of them ex-KLM aircraft, and First Air has been very happy with their performance so far. Two of them were converted to combi aircraft before joining the airline and one, C-FFNC, is flying in an all-passenger version. The Boeing 737-400s are mainly used on the trunk routes from southern Canada up to Iqaluit, Kuujjuaq and Yellowknife. Interestingly, when the Boeing 737-400s were introduced, First Air got some complaints about the aircraft's noise level — or the lack thereof. For many locals from the small northern communities, when they heard the aircraft land in their town, that was the time they would leave for the airport to catch their flight or pick somebody up there. With the much quieter Boeing 737-400s, they often could hear the aircraft land any more.

First Air's biggest aircraft type ever, a single Boeing 767-200 freighter registered C-GKLY, was recently removed from First Air's AOC, mostly due to the high costs involved with operating a fleet of just one aircraft. The aircraft, now in neutral white colours, has been transferred to Cargojet Airlines, a Canadian cargo airline operating a much bigger fleet of Boeing 767s and 757s. After the transfer, the aircraft still operates on an ACMI contract on behalf of First Air on the airline's cargo routes from Winnipeg and Ottawa to Iqaluit and Kuujjuaq.

And then there are two exotics in the fleet: both of Canada's only civilian Lockheed L-100-30 Hercules aircraft, based at Yellowknife. They usually operate charter flights on behalf of the many mining companies doing business in Canada's north, but are also available for other missions. Just recently, one of them was chartered by an American airline to bring a Boeing 777 engine from the US to the island of Bermuda, immediately followed by another engine transport to the Dominican Republic. Quite an exciting trip for a Hercules crew usually flying mining charters from their base at Yellowknife! The two versatile Hercules also assisted in the aftermath of the devastating earthquake in Haiti, when much-needed supplies were flown there. Just recently, First Air became the first airline in the world to equip all of its Boeing 737s and ATRs with the Canadian-built FLYHTStream system, allowing livestreaming of the aircraft black box data to the ground via satellite. Operating in some of the world's harshest conditions, maintenance staff on the ground will have easy access to the aircraft's vital data, should any irregularities occur.

VFR (visiting friends and relatives), government, and business traffic (mining industry for example) are key to the success at First Air but a niche that generates a steady stream of revenue as well are medical contracts. Most of the small communities in the north have only very limited medical facilities. Thus, passengers often travel to the bigger cities like Iqaluit or Yellowknife or even further south to seek medical treatments. Airlines are requested to bid for medical contract work with the local governments on certain routes and once they secure such a contract can accrue quite steady additional revenue through medical travel. The downside of these contracts is that a certain number of weekly and sometimes daily frequencies has to be operated on the particular route, which is often more than demand would justify.

First Air also operates many specialised charters. All major mining companies in the north are regular customers of First Air and they require the entire fleet of the airline on a daily basis: ATRs, gravel-equipped Boeing 737s, and the two Hercules all operate on charter services regularly.

The cost of operating in Canada's north is horrendous, which explains the very expensive fares on First Air flights. Unlike in other countries, air transport is not subsidised (as it is in Europe through Public Service Obligation routes, Essential Air Services in the United States, or other schemes) airlines have to be self-sufficient. Until 2010,

First Air was profitable and it was only in the last few years that the impact of the global economic downturn started hitting the airline's bottom line and the carrier operated at a loss. Right now, the airline finds itself in a major restructuring programme, led by a new management team appointed in 2013, including CEO Brock Friesen and Vice President Commercial Bert van der Stege.

As with most airlines around the world these days, reducing costs was one of the prime targets and some major reductions have been achieved through renegotiations of contracts with suppliers. Close to 300 projects are currently under way and as Bert van der Stege explains: "We are questioning ourselves every day: what we are doing, how we are running our business, and constantly asking ourselves if there is a better and more efficient way." The objective of the new management team's efforts is to reach breakeven for 2014, become fully profitable again in 2015, and start expansion in 2016 in order to benefit from the economies of scale of a growing operation. More fuel-efficient aircraft is also on the agenda and thus, possible replacements for the Boeing 737-200s will be sought more seriously.

Another goal is better fleet utilisation. The Boeing 737-400s, for example, usually depart from airports in southern Canada in the morning, fly up to Iqaluit or Yellowknife, return in the late afternoon and go to sleep for the next twelve hours or so — time in which they could very well be used on charter flights, even to Florida or the Caribbean, or other activities generating additional revenue.

In order to achieve cost savings and make the entire operation in the north more sustainable, a merger with First Air's biggest competitor, Canadian North, is currently being negotiated. Canadian North is owned by the NorTerra Group and operates a network very similar to First Air's with a fleet of Boeing 737-200s and Dash 8s. Because the two airlines networks' similar structure, flights on the same route often depart at the same or very similar times, i.e. early morning departures from southern gateways like Ottawa or Edmonton to the North and similar connecting flights from there. More than often, both airlines would operate their flights only half full, so the positive impact that a joint operation would have for their balance sheet is thus very obvious.

In the opinion of industry observers and stakeholders of both airlines, neither of the two airlines will be sustainable individually, at least not in the long run, and that is why a merger of the two carriers is currently being discussed. The outcome of this, as this article goes to press, is still open. To describe what First Air means for the communities in the north as absolutely vital is no exaggeration. Not too long ago, travel options and the access of goods and services to the small communities in Canada's north were very limited. There is no road and rail link between most towns in the north and major Canadian cities, so safe and reliable air transportation is absolutely essential for them to survive. With its comprehensive network and daily flights on most routes, First Air can ensure that important equipment, mail and other goods can make it from southern Canada to even the most remote outstations within one day. First Air, carrying approximately 260,000 passengers and in excess of thirty million kilograms of freight and mail around its network, plays a vital part for the communities in Canada's north, and no matter what the outcome of the merger talks with Canadian North, will continue doing so in the future.

First Air is a perfect example of how an airline can make even the world's most remote places accessible. Look on their route map. They fly to Cambridge Bay, Inuvik, Pond Inlet. Find those places on a map. You almost can't be further away from civilisation (admittedly the definition of 'civilisation' may have to be discussed) and they even serve you a hot breakfast while flying you there on time. What airlines like First Air do is simply breathtaking. Flying passengers from London to Berlin or New York to L.A. may be something. Bringing them up to Resolute Bay and still delivering a safe and on-time performance is something else. And after some quite painful restructuring, First Air even turns a profit now, not even having merged with Canadian North. Quite an amazing airline. One of my favourites. Hats off!

Nature Air — Costa Rica's Remarkable Little Airline

(appeared in Airliner World February 2013)

Costa Rica in Central America is one of the world's most diverse countries (in particular considering its small size), offering visitors active volcanoes, dense rainforest or beautiful beaches. Most visitors come here for the amazing nature and the country is keenly supporting ecotourism, not mass tourism as found in other parts of the region. It is no coincidence that the name of one of the most interesting airlines in the area is Nature Air. The airline, founded some twenty years ago, has become the country's leading domestic airline covering all major cities and tourist destinations in the country, and also the largest charter operator in Central America.

Nature Air would not be what it is today without one man: its founder and owner Alex Khajavi. Based in California and with a background in international finance, he was working on a consulting project in 2000, advising a little local airline in Costa Rica with just one Britten-Norman Islander, Travelair.

Travelair at the time was providing a number of domestic flights around the country but not doing too well. Alex Khajavi, with no airline background whatsoever, looked at the airline purely from a financial and marketing perspective and realised that its business model was actually very promising, the airline just wasn't run very well.

At the time, there were hardly any reliable airlines to transport tourists between the major tourist sights or locals from smaller communities to the capital. Overland travel often took very long, was not comfortable and sometimes unsafe, so there was definitely a need for a reliable domestic operation. A number of foreign investors were willing to take over the little airline and re-start it, but could not agree on ownership questions and eventually abandoned the plan, with the future looking dim.

Still believing in the project, Alex Khajavi teamed up with two investors to buy the airline just before September 11, 2001. After the events in New York, the other two investors backed out of the project, leaving Alex Khajavi as the only one. He decided to move ahead no matter what, sold some property in California, bought Travelair and moved to Costa Rica.

Ever since its relaunch as Nature Air, the airline has been growing rapidly and became one of the most successful companies in the region. Today, Alex Khajavi is still the owner and CEO of Nature Air and not only the airline but a number of companies assembled under the Nature Group umbrella. The group includes Nature Air, travel company Nature Vacations, flying school Aerotica, consulting firm Naturegate, and Naturekids, a non-profit organisation providing affordable and high-quality education for children in more remote parts of the country.

A look at the last pages of the airline's Landings inflight magazine reveals a lovingly illustrated route network that covers thirteen destinations within Costa Rica and two international routes, Managua in Nicaragua and Bocas del Toro in Panama. Its main base is Tobías Bolaños airport, the smaller of the two international airports of the capital San José. While Costa Rica is not a big country, driving times can be quite long. Driving from San José to the coastal towns of Puerto Jímenez or Golfito in the south of the country can easily take seven or eight hours. Add to that heavy rain or the occasional landslide and a flight of just forty-five minutes seems like a very attractive option in comparison. With much-reduced travel times by taking a flight, tourists are able to see more places in Costa Rica within the limited time they often have. On most of its routes, Nature Air carries a good mix of tourists and locals, their respective share depending on the season. During the low season, when touristic demand is lower, the number of flights is reduced or destinations are combined with each other to make flying more viable.

Nature Air also does what a number of airlines in Europe have started doing: it shares aircraft with other operators or leases them from them. It has entered agreements with Grand Canyon Airlines, Scenic Airlines and Twin Otter International and, as luck would have it, the high season in Costa Rica is when the demand is low in the United States and vice versa. Thus, Nature Air increases the size of its fleet during the busiest time of the year and has no excess aircraft standing around during the quieter months.

Apart from scheduled flying, charters are an important part of

Nature Air's operation. Not only are tourist groups flown around the country and region, Nature Air also has long-standing relationships with numerous non-governmental organisations and scientific institutions operating in the country and operates flights on their behalf regularly. In 2011, the airline flew more than 110,000 passengers around the region, a figure which takes a while to reach when you use Twin Otters and Cessna Caravans.

Sustainability may be a term which has been overstrained in recent years by almost all kinds of companies, not only airlines. While often it seems to be a marketing tool more than anything else, sustainability really is a key component of how Nature Air is run and things seem to run a little deeper here, something which is of high importance to Alex Khajavi. One of the prime targets are CO_2 emissions. As early as 2004, the airline decided to offset 100% of the CO_2 emissions caused by its flights and became the world's first certified carbon-neutral airline. Unlike other carriers, it does not offer passengers a voluntary scheme that they can decide to pay into but simply offsets all its emissions.

Since the carbon offset programme started, nearly 1000 acres of land are sponsored annually, thus protected from the deforestation they would otherwise face and are conserved for the future. Most of the money goes directly to landowners as a supplementary income, in return for which they pledge to maintain standing forests on their property, while other farms pledge reforestation. The airline also tries to become more efficient itself and fuel burn reductions of seven percent have been achieved in the last three years through minimising aircraft weight, or better flight planning. The acquisition of a new aircraft type, the Cessna 208, was also decided in order to bring fuel burn down, as Alex Khajavi explains. "We have a number of thinner routes or charter flights which are not fully booked. Although we are generally very happy with the performance of the Twin Otters, in terms of fuel burn it still does not make much sense to fly six or seven empty seats around constantly on certain routes or certain times of the day, neither financially nor from an environmental point of view."

Sustainability also plays an important role in the way Nature Air treats its employees, offers them opportunities and tries to keep experienced staff in the company. A number of the airline's pilots, for example, have started their career with the airline as check-in staff or baggage handlers. Since one of the companies that is part of the Nature Group is a flying school, Aerotica, also located at Tobías Bolaños Airport, candidates that were interested were offered attractive conditions for their pilot training. They were able to continue their previous work with Nature Air parallel to their pilot training. The result: a highly motivated and loyal workforce that might not be looking for the first opportunity to leave the airline and start working elsewhere.

Nature Air has ambitious plans and some of them may have become a reality at the time this article goes to press. As of now, the airline operates a fleet of Twin Otters and Cessna Caravans (all painted in different, beautiful colours) on what is mostly a domestic network. The only two international destinations are Bocas del Toro in Panama and Managua, the capital of neighbouring Nicaragua. For these rather short routes, the Twin Otter or Caravan may be the right kind of aircraft, yet Alex Khajavi sees a lot of room for future expansion. "We are looking at expanding into neighbouring countries that only see limited or not very convenient service from San José. The major carriers in the region, Copa and TACA, do provide plenty of service around the region. But the timings are often not very convenient if you don't want to connect elsewhere through their hubs. Point-to-point traffic around the region is fairly underdeveloped and if it exists, it is prohibitively expensive."

Possible future expansion includes key business routes like the existing one to Managua, which would see additional frequencies and shorter flight times than currently on the Twin Otter, or Panama City, where Nature Air plans to serve Albrook Airport, much closer to the city than Tocumen International. What Nature Air does now within Costa Rica would also be replicated internationally: allow tourists to combine the highlights of the region within one trip more easily, so a number of more touristy destinations are also likely to become part of Nature Air's network expansion.

The number of fliers in Costa Rica and neighbouring countries is still very low. People are used to travelling long distances by bus. Some math by Alex Khajavi: "If I want to travel from San José to Panama City by bus, that would take me around fifteen hours and cost approximately $50 [USD] for a comfortable first class ticket. En route, I would probably buy some food or something to drink, so let us add another $10 to $20 for that and we get close to $70 oneway. Now, if Nature Air offered a oneway flight for say $90 or $100 on that route, people would have to pay a little bit more, but save fourteen hours of travelling time." He is convinced that with a great product, convenient timing and sufficient frequencies, he could lure a good percentage of present bus travellers (and maybe non-travellers) onto a Nature Air flight and adds: "We are not going to eat anything away from TACA or Copa, as most of their traffic is connecting traffic, not point-to-point. We are after the top twenty percent of the bus travellers."

The strategy for the to-be-launched international flights to be successful sounds quite simple: attractive timing and frequencies, point-to-point service to untapped or underserved markets, and lower fares than they are currently offered. International flights may start sooner rather than later and negotiations with investors from abroad are in their final stages. An aircraft type has already been finalised: the Saab 340. This type is a comfortable turboprop, has the right size to start up international flights and is available in sufficient numbers at reasonable leasing terms. "We were very interested in the DHC8-300, also because of the chance to later possibly upgrade to the bigger DHC8-400, but the market is currently quite empty and prices have gone up considerably, making this unattractive for us at the time being."

It is also not yet decided whether the operations of these international flights would also take place from Tobías Bolaños airport (SYQ), Nature Air's current base, or Juan Santamaria International (SJO), further outside the city (which is also where its only domestic competitor SANSA is based). While many passengers like the proximity to the city and small airport convenience that Tobías Bolaños offers, it does not have any connectivity elsewhere.

Yet, at its home base, Nature Air is the only scheduled airline, giving it a good position in terms of flight operations. From here, the airline can schedule flights at their liking and rarely faces any delays. By contrast, there are many other airlines at SJO, in particular TACA who have a big operation there. Nature Air's flights would compete for access at busy times of the day. Furthermore, it remains unclear as of now, from which terminal Nature Air would operate or if they would build their own building. Alex points out that Nature Air would probably move a good part of their operation to SJO if the conditions were right, although he expects to leave some domestic flying at Tobías Bolaños airport no matter what, as the airport is hugely popular, in particular with business travellers living nearby who would have a much longer commute to the international airport.

A flight on Nature Air is a pleasant and memorable experience. At Tobías Bolaños airport check-in is very efficient. There is a little waiting lounge with TV, free wireless internet and complimentary coffee. A few minutes before departure, travellers are taken into a little room to watch a safety video, in which children that have been supported through the Nature Kids programme take passengers through the safety procedures. Rather sweet to watch! After the video, the captain comes to pick passengers up and accompany them for the short walk across the apron to the waiting aircraft.

Although Nature Air also offers special scenic flights around the volcanoes and pristine landscape that Costa Rica offers, most scheduled flights also involve a fair bit of sightseeing, as the Twin Otters and Caravans do not fly very high and there is almost always a volcano or otherwise stunning scenery en route. For those who cannot get enough or have little time to spend and want to see a lot of places, Nature Air offers an air pass with unlimited flying for one or two weeks, starting from $282 [USD] during the low season. The Twin Otter Vistaliners with their big windows offer great views and once more, the airline's care for little details shows, as windows are cleaned before flights to allow for perfect viewing and photography.

Even though the airline has ambitious expansion plans, Alex Khajavi says he is an advocate of what he calls "gentle walking". He does not want a rushed expansion at any price but is ready to take advantage of growing opportunities when they arise. It will be exciting to follow the developments at this remarkable Costa Rican airline.

Don't you just adore people who quit their job, sell their house and move to another country because they want to start something completely new? I absolutely do. I am German. We love our security and if we can, we stay with a job for our entire life, just because it's safe and there is no risk involved. This article is about a brave man who left his old life. He took the risk, moved to Costa Rica and bought a tiny airline because he believed in what they were doing (and saw what this small airline could be turned into). And Nature Air became a whopping success. It is still a small airline today but definitely one with some of the most beautiful looking aircraft, all painted in different colour schemes. Alex Khajavi — such a nice and friendly man — got rewarded for taking a risk and this fact alone makes it worth writing about Nature Air.

Shizuoka - Mount Fuji's own airport

(appeared in Airliner World June 2010)

Japan is a country with lots and lots of infrastructure — and that includes many airports great and small, linking even the smallest cities to the country's metropolises. Quite recently, another airport has been added to the collection: Mount Fuji Shizuoka Airport. The brand-new airport (IATA: FSZ, ICAO: RJNS) is located on a high plateau around twenty-seven kilometres (seventeen miles) from the city of Shizuoka in the prefecture of the same name. Mount Fuji, the holy mountain of the Japanese and patron of the airport, is around eighty kilometres (fifty miles) away from the terminal, perfectly visible on a clear day.

The new airport was originally scheduled to open in March 2009, but was delayed by the shortening of the single runway 12/30 from 2,500 metres (8,202 feet) to 2,200 metres (7,218 feet) by the implementation of a displaced threshold which cannot be used for take-off or landing due to environmental and noise concerns, thus a reduction of the already built infrastructure. After some months of delay, the airport eventually opened on June 4, 2009.

The airport has all the amenities you would expect of a new airport. The small terminal has a central check-in area, located on the ground floor, which is used by all airlines, domestic and international. A number of car rental agencies are complemented by an information counter, staffed by Japanese ladies in traditional attire, and a little supermarket. The ground floor is not only the check-in area but also the arrivals zone, a design that can be found at most smaller Japanese airports. The first floor has a large shop selling almost everything you could imagine including a wide range of food. There is also an exhibition about the airport and the Shizuoka region. The first floor is the departure level and passengers with their boarding passes pass through security here.

The entire terminal is well-lit, with a large glass front stretching all the way up above the main entrance and a part-glass ceiling. Another escalator leads up to the second floor. Here a cafeteria-style restaurant offers Japanese and international food of good quality at affordable prices. And then, is there a Japanese airport without one? a large observation deck offering views of the main apron, the runway and — on a clear day — Mount Fuji in the background. The observation deck is either glazed or fenced off, but photo holes allow for decent photography. Most airlines use one of the two jetways the airport has and passengers can reach the additional aircraft parking stands on foot easily.

A large, car park provides space for around 2,550 vehicles free of charge. The airport is connected to the cities around it by bus, including Shizuoka, Kakegawa and Hamamatsu as well as Nagoya international airport. Ironically, one of Japan's main train lines, the Shinkansen between Tokyo and Nagoya, passes right underneath the airport but Japan Railways decided not to build a proper airport station (maybe to protect itself from another competitor?).

As of early 2010, a surprising variety of airlines are offering services from Shizuoka Airport. Both Koreanair and Asiana Airlines offer a daily connection to Seoul's Incheon Airport, using Boeing 737s and Airbus A321s. The Koreanair flight has a codeshare with Japan Airlines and a similar arrangement exists between Asiana and ANA. China Eastern Airlines provides two weekly flights to Shanghai Pudong, usually bringing in Airbus A320s.

Domestically, All Nippon Airways offers a daily flight from Sapporo on the island of Hokkaido in the north of Japan. After arrival from Sapporo, the aircraft, usually a Boeing 737-700, continues to the holiday island of Okinawa. In the late afternoon, it returns from there and flies on back to Sapporo. Japan Airlines subsidiary J-Air provides another daily connection to Sapporo and three daily trips to Fukuoka in southwest Japan using Embraer 170s, although the airline has announced to withdraw services from the airport after April 1st, 2010.

The star among the airlines flying to Shizuoka is actually based here and only started operations after the airport had opened, in July 2009: Fuji Dream Airlines. As of now, Fuji Dream Airlines operates two colourful Embraer 170s, one in a bright red, the second in a light blue colour scheme on two daily flights to Komatsu, just forty minutes flying time to the north side of Honshu, the main island forming Japan, and one daily trip to Kagoshima and Kumamoto on Kyushu Island in southwest Japan. Fuji Dream plans to add a third aircraft (possibly a larger Embraer 175) and with the cessation of JAL flights it seems likely that Fuji Dream might take over at least one of JAL's destinations.

Some more airlines serve the airport with charter flights. China Airlines visits up to two times per week from Taipei and Taiwanese carriers EVA Air and Mandarin have offered occasional flights to Shizuoka in the past, as has China Southern Airlines. Just after the opening of Shizuoka Airport, Edelweiss Air from Switzerland included the airport in its summer charter programme of flights from various Japanese Airports to Switzerland, and landed here with an Airbus A330.

Located right between Tokyo and Nagoya, you could ask if this new airport is really needed. Anybody from the Shizuoka prefecture who has flown from the new local airport and no doubt found this facility very convenient will tell you it is! It will never become an international hub like its neighbours — the rather short runway and small terminal simply don't allow it. Nevertheless, for flights to the neighbouring countries of Korea, China and Taiwan, the airport has already found its niche despite the announcement of Japan Airlines withdrawal of their domestic flights.

Having its own local airline with additional aircraft on order should generate further growth and new routes for the airport in the near future, and while the Japanese majors like ANA and JAL concentrate on their existing hubs, the acquisition of a low-cost airline like Skymark (already quite successful at the new Kobe Airport near Osaka) may bring in additional traffic.

From an enthusiast's point of view, this airport is almost perfect. As well as the observation deck, on both sides of the terminal area, there are viewing areas that are easily accessible and offer even better opportunities for viewing and photography. Those two spots, however, are very exposed to the elements, so on a cold, windy January day (as experienced by the author) it can get very chilly there. Both vantage points are easily reached on foot and you can see both of them from the observation deck (usually both of them are 'staffed' by local spotters). Traffic is not brisk but with a good mix of airlines it hardly ever gets boring. The greatest attraction of the airport is of course Fuji Dream Airlines, an airline you don't see at the big airports of Japan. The busiest time of the day is between nine in the morning and one in the afternoon;

happily this is when the light is perfect for photography. And when the airport is not busy for a while, why not stroll down the small path from the viewing point at the eastern end and visit the beautiful monastery nearby, a very peaceful place indeed!

All the people who know me, know what a big fan of Japan I am. For me, Japan is the perfect country. It is very clean, very organised, everyone is polite, mobile phones are forbidden on the train (great!) and the trains always leave on time. I come to Japan as often as I can. For someone who likes to watch and photograph airplanes, it doesn't get any better. All airports have beautiful observation decks and take really good care of aviation enthusiasts. This airport here, Shizuoka, even has Mount Fuji in the background on a clear day, Japan's holy mountain. And one of the nicest looking airlines, Fuji Dream Airlines, calls Shizuoka home. All of their Embraer jets wear different colours. A dream! That's why I wanted to have this article in the book. Plus — I really love Japan. Have I mentioned it?

Region Avia

(appeared in Airliner World February 2009)

In the vastness of Russia, it can take many hours simply to get from one city to the next — even if you're travelling by air! A flight from Moscow to the Russian Far East can easily take longer than the average transatlantic trip. When the Soviet Union existed, numerous subsidised air services offered a link to the rest of the empire — or at least the nearest big city — for even the smallest communities. Small aircraft, such as the Antonov An-2 or the more comfortable Let-410, often operated these flights. During the 1990s economic crisis, many of these routes were closed, carriers ceased operations and the many newly independent airlines focussed on more promising ventures. Without government-subsidised tickets, most villagers in remote communities couldn't afford the fare.

In a region like Yakutia, in the far east of Russia, lack of air services mean being cut-off from the outside world for about six months a year because of the weather, although not in the season you might think. In winter, when everything is frozen and temperatures can drop to minus 60°C, it's actually easier to drive long distances — it's in summer when the problems arise. Many of the rivers become vast, impassable currents.

However, the economic situation in Russia has improved significantly in recent years so growing numbers of people can afford to travel — and do. Revitalising neglected air links is one way of creating a better infrastructure and many regions are trying to entice airlines to operate on remote routes.

Moscow-based Region Avia Airlines is one airline trying to capitalise on the rising demand for air travel within the regions. Its CEO, Denis Pavshinsky, explained that the biggest potential for the airlines lies far away from the capital, in regions like Yakutia, Kamchatka or around Magadan. The name "Region Avia" says it all; many of the bigger Russian cities are quite well linked (primarily to Moscow and increasingly to each other). Smaller communities, however, are often still cut off from the rest of the world. Travelling to them takes many hours by road which can sometimes be completely impossible.

Region Avia aims to re-establish links to these communities and has successfully launched operations in some of Russia's most isolated places. The airline is privately owned (forty-five percent of the shares are held by the European Bank of Reconstruction and Development (EBRD) through its investment fund Norum). Russian investors hold the remainder. The airline is included in the Government of Moscow's programme to develop regional passenger services in the Central Federal District and has been granted a credit of $6.3 million.

The carrier's aircraft of choice is the Ukrainian-built Antonov An-28, a very robust small turboprop commuter seating up to seventeen passengers. It can operate from the smallest of airports that could otherwise be reached only by helicopter. It combines relative comfort and excellent STOL performance with low operating costs. Its one drawback is availability — during the Perestroika period of the late 1980s and onwards, aircraft development was not a priority. The airline would like to extend the fleet, because business opportunities for a niche operator in this vast country are almost endless, but the limited number of aircraft built and the high demand for them, particularly in Africa, makes it difficult to source additional machines at short notice. After Region Avia's launch in 2007 in Kamchatka, Karelia and Yakutia, the fleet grew to eight aircraft the following year including five based at the airport of Magan, just a few miles away from the city of Yakutsk, the capital of Yakutia province. The creation of an aerial link means a huge improvement in living conditions and economic prospects for isolated areas.

Region Avia's operation in Yakutia runs year-round, bringing a viable alternative to travellers who prefer an hour in the air to ten in a car. While ticket prices in such a remote part of the world are generally high, the airline tries to keep them attractively priced. The carrier receives significant support from the airports and currently doesn't pay landing fees, which helps keep fares down.

Two An-28s were initially based at Magan and carried 10,000 passengers in the first year, most of whom had never flown before. Carrying that many people on seventeen-seaters also meant a lot of flights. While the acceptance of air service was slow during the first months of operations, awareness of the available services increased significantly and many people now choose to fly.

The author's first flight in Yakutia was in July 2008, on the airline's busiest route in the province, from Magan to the small town of Ust-Maya near the confluence of the Aldan and Maya rivers and unreachable by road during summer because of impassable waterways en route.

Magan airport is about nine miles (fifteen kilometres) from Yakutsk city centre and is one of the city's two airports, the other being Yakutsk International Airport which is closer to the city centre. Magan has traditionally been the centre for general aviation and regional flights and sits on a plateau above the city. Its higher location means it is unaffected by the spring floods, which can severely affect operations at the lower Yakutsk International.

Arriving at the airport for the morning departure, I was surprised to see a very small, modern terminal. A new holding company — Aeroporti Severa, Airports of the North — has recently been formed, bringing under one roof a number of tiny, small and medium-sized airports in the province. Owned and controlled by the Russian federal government, its goal is to improve the infrastructure at small airports. Major funding has resulted in upgraded facilities at existing airports that in some cases have not seen scheduled service for almost two decades.

Check-in is swift and efficient. Passengers are directed to the departure lounge where they wait for the bus transfer to the aircraft, together with piles of lugagge (including boxes of mayonnaise, fruit, tools etc). Just ten minutes before the scheduled departure, passengers for Ust-Maya board the bus for the minute's drive across the unpaved apron to the waiting An-28, RA-28900.

It is a lovely summer's day with temperatures close to 30°C; it's hard to imagine what it must be like during winter, when temperatures are among the lowest in the world. The enormous annual temperature variances make it difficult to build roads, houses or virtually anything. Asphalt usually cracks during the winter and even the most carefully paved road will be in poor shape a year later. That's why many airport runways or aprons remain unprepared. Gravel strips are just much less sensitive to the harsh conditions and aircraft like the An-28 or An-2 can operate easily from them.

Magan Airport is the hub for Region Avia in Yakutia. Five aircraft are based here and depart in an almost star-shaped pattern in the morning and late afternoon (all operations are VFR only). A typical sector is around 300 miles (500 kilometres) in length. After boarding via the rear stairs and climbing past the luggage storage area, our flight to Ust-Maya departs on time and the aircraft is almost fully booked with sixteen passengers plus cargo loaded both in the rear and forward cabins.

As the An-28 does not have a pressurised cabin, cruising altitude does not exceed 10,000 feet (3,000 metres). The landscape below is very green, with many small lakes. After an hour, the crew starts the descent into Ust-Maya, a small airport built during World War Two. The gravel runway is 3,576 ft (1,090 m) long and has accommodated aircraft up to the size of an An-12. Yakutsk can be reached from the town by road from November until April, although the journey can take from six to twelve hours; it's impossible to reach the regional capital by road in summer.

After we have disembarked, luggage and cargo are offloaded and the aircraft is ready for the return flight to Yakutsk. Because an additional flight had been scheduled for the afternoon, I was able to spend a couple of hours in this beautiful area. The director of Ust-Maya's airport, Dmitri Katkov, gave me a short tour of the facility. He explained the enormous positive impact of the flights for local people, saving them lengthy trips by Jeep or boat. Goods can be brought in and out more easily, and people taken to a doctor in case of a medical emergency. The first tourists had been welcomed in the area and more were expected.

The airport is quite basic, with people waiting for the flight to Magan sitting in the open-air waiting lounge, which resembles a little garden outside the wooden building. The return flight to Magan takes just over an hour and most passengers doze off shortly after take-off.

The next day, I took a flight to Aldan, which seems to have been important enough an airport in the past to have an IATA three-letter code assigned to it: ADH. The flight time is just over one and a half hours. Two Yakovlev Yak-40s, stored in very poor condition, are a reminder of the airport's past glory. A few days before my visit, the city had been surrounded by forest fires and one of Region Avia's aircraft helped in the fire fighting by carrying equipment to Aldan.

Until now, all of Region Avia's services have been point-to-point and serve outlying cities, mostly in Russia's far east. However, the airline plans to become a feeder to the country's bigger aviation hubs. While the fleet of An-28s will stay in operation (simply because there is no real alternative), there are plans to bring significant growth and new travel options to potential passengers. Several turboprop aircraft have been evaluated and a number of Embraer EMB-120 Brasilias have been acquired to start a new 'branch' of Region Avia. According to Alexey Marchukov, commercial director for Region Avia, it is the right size for this type of operation — opening up new routes — and aircraft like the ATR 42 or Bombardier Dash 8 would be more difficult to fill. This new operation will start from Moscow and link cities within a 620 mile (1,000 km) radius of one of the capital's airports — probably either Domodedovo or Vnukovo. Marchukov explained that Domodedovo is the best in terms of international connectivity, while Vnukovo is owned by the Moscow city government, which is very keen to create fast links to cities on the periphery that can currently only be reached by car. The congested roads around Moscow mean that it can take up to six hours to travel 90 miles (150 km) by car.

With an initial fleet of seven EMB-120s, Region Avia aims to fly to cities like Ivanovo (where a new airport has just opened), Petrozavodsk or Yoshkar-Ola (the capital of the Mari El Republic). All are within 620 miles (1,000 km) of Moscow and don't have scheduled air service or are under-served. Operations to Yoshkar-Ola and Ivanovo have already started from Vnukovo, even before the first Embraer has been delivered. For the transitional period, a co-operation agreement has been signed with Volga-Dnepr Airlines, which operates the flights with Yak-40s.

Other cities that may soon be added when Region Avia's own operations are up and running include Ulyanovsk, Lipetsk, Cheboksary, Pensa or Saransk. There are plans for regional air hubs like Ekaterinburg, Novosibirsk, Samara and others to be linked to smaller centres around them. The airline aims to operate twenty Embraers within the next three years, while the An-28 operations, a significant and stable contributor to the financial results, will continue in the far east.

There are plans for interline agreements with bigger airlines for the feeder flights into larger airports — for smooth onward connections both ways. Ticket sales are currently handled by the standard travel agencies and the Russian *aviakassi*, the airline ticket offices found in even smaller cities. The company plans to add e-tickets and internet purchase to the existing mix. Region Avia has done a remarkable job in the niche market that it operates. It will now be interesting to see if the business model is transferable to larger markets and aircraft.

Region Avia for me was another perfect example of how airlines can make people's lives better — and I am not talking about affordable fares to Bangkok here. Remote regions of the world, be it in Siberia, Northern Canada, Easter Island or other far away places completely rely on aviation. Airplanes bring in the daily supplies, anything from fresh milk and vegetables to toothpaste and toilet paper. They take sick people to hospital or bring in a doctor. In the case of Region Avia, people's lives in the small Siberian communities really improved a lot with the launch of flights. They were able to travel to the nearest big city year round easily, had better access to the outside world. Tourism flourished in some places and everybody I asked said their lives had generally improved a lot. Region Avia also made my life better because I travelled to Yakutia to visit them. What a beautiful part of the world that is! Unfortunately, and it is beyond my understanding why this venture failed, Region Avia was liquidated in 2011, leaving a number of communities without a regular and fast connection to the outside world once more. They probably miss it. But who knows, maybe one day an innovative airline sees the niche Region Avia has left behind.

"The Doctor is in!" — on a Daytrip to the Arctic Circle
(appeared in Airways July 2012)

As an aviation enthusiast keen on collecting airlines and aircraft, you can plan your little flights and daytrips as fastidiously as you want. Suddenly, for whatever reason, everything takes a different turn and you end up somewhere else than planned, fly on different airplanes or end up staying put where you wanted to start from. This was one of those days.

While on a holiday trip to Iceland and Greenland in September 2010, plans called for a daytrip from the Icelandic capital Reykjavik, flying up to the town of Akureyri and further on to the small volcanic island of Grimsey on Norlandair's bright red Twin Otter. Norlandair 'inherited' Air Iceland's Akureyri section and their pair of Twin Otters when they were retired a few years ago. After a few minutes on the ground in Grimsey, the same routing would bring us back to the capital Reykjavik, with just a few hours in Akureyri in between flights.

Things started with an early morning walk from the hotel to Reykjavik's charming downtown airport. Low fences, no security control for domestic flights, an interesting variety of based aircraft and often unusual visitors make any visit to this airport worthwhile and easy for passengers. Today's special was a Swiss DC-3 nightstopping here en route to the United States. Reykjavik to Akureyri is the busiest domestic route in Iceland and usually served by Air Iceland's Fokker 50s; sometimes their smaller Dash 8s also fly there. Of course, my flights were carefully selected in order to sample the Dash 8 on the way to Akureyri and the Fokker 50 on the way back to Reykjavik in the afternoon.

A quick forty minute flight brought us to Akureyri, where the approach is over quite spectacular mountain scenery towards the small airport of the city. Like the town itself, Akureyri Airport (AEY/BIAR) is located in the delta of the Eyjafjörður fjord that flows into the Greenland Sea north of Akureyri. During the flight from Reykjavik, grey, overcast weather had changed to clear blue skies. In Akureyri, we had three hours to spend. Enough time for a walk into town along the fjord. A friend of mine, born and raised (and traumatised, he insisted) in Akureyri, warned me: "This is the most boring place on earth. It is terrible!" Turned out Akureyri is quite a pleasant city, probably not the most exciting but definitely fine to walk around in for a few hours on a sunny day; soon it was time to walk back to the airport for my connecting flight to the volcanic island of Grimsey.

However, at the Norlandair check-in counter, we were told that our stay on the island was to be quite a bit longer today. Today was the day that a doctor travelled to the island to see his local patients there. As no doctor permanently resides on Grimsey, he travels over once a month to see all patients in one go. These multiple doctor appointments can, depending on demand and severity, take anywhere from a few minutes to a few hours each. Fine with us, as it was a sunny day and we had no other plans.

Also quite newsworthy was an aircraft change that we noticed soon later. As Norlandair's Twin Otter was needed elsewhere (the airline operates three scheduled routes from Akureyri, in addition to charter flights that have taken the Twin Otters as far as Greenland or Spitzbergen), our flight was to be operated by a Piper PA-31 instead, chartered from Myflug, another small local airline. Again, not bad news really, as I had never flown on that type before.

With a total of five passengers on board, one of them an elderly man returning home from heart surgery on the mainland, we departed for Grimsey minutes later. Taking off towards the south, the Piper performed a steep 180-degree turn and continued along the fjord and over very quiet waters towards the Greenland Sea. Grimsey, a tiny island measuring just 5.3 square kilometers (just over two square miles), is the northernmost inhabited territory of Iceland and sits right on the Arctic Circle. It is home to around one hundred inhabitants and up to a million seabirds (depending on the season).

People living on Grimsey are among Iceland's more well-off. There is no crime and no police and nobody is without work. Fishing is the major industry and it has made people here very wealthy in the past decades. After twenty-four minutes in the air, never exceeding 3,000 feet, we touched down on runway 18 of Grimsey's airport (GRY/BIGR).

The station manager met the flight (it later turned out she also helps in the local shop and takes care of the church garden as the airport alone would not keep her busy). She told us that we could expect a minimum of three hours on the island and told us, "Be back at two!" The tiny village starts right next to the airport but first of all, we needed to check out the island's main attraction: the Arctic Circle. It crosses the island right next to the small airport terminal and there is even a small monument and photo platform. Also, every passenger taking the flight to Grimsey is automatically issued a Polar Circle certificate by Norlandair, a nice gesture by the airline. The day continued to be bright and sunny and so I enjoyed walking up and down the 'High Street' a bit. Eventually, I ended up at the island's little church. It is so small, you could not describe it. One could hardly stand upright in it — like a little doll's house.

The church gardener (a.k.a. the airport station manager) told us it was going to be a little longer, a rake in her hand and taking care of the church garden at the same time. 3pm was the latest estimated departure time, giving us some more time to explore the little island. Life here seems to be quite comfortable, houses are very cozy and the island even has a soccer pitch and an indoor swimming pool. The public doctor's appointment, by the way, took place at the local school.

Some more walking around, an extensive shopping spree at the island's small shop and I made my way back to the airport. After another half hour wait and more pictures being taken of the Arctic Circle, eventually, at 3.30pm, the doctor arrived, as did the remaining three passengers booked on the flight. Boarding took a minute and we were on our way back to Akureyri. Our connecting flight back to Reykjavik? "All taken care of, don't worry!"

Just over twenty minutes of flying brought us back to Akureyri. The alternative to flying (daily in the summer months, three times a week in winter) is an often rough three-hour ferry ride. An easy choice, it seems. Back in Akureyri, an Air Iceland agent met us and handed over our new boarding passes for a later flight to Reykjavik that we had been re-booked on. There would even have been time to explore the Icelandic Aviation Museum at the airport, but unfortunately it was closed and only the front section of a DC-6 and the airworthy DC-3 parked outside could be seen. Boarding time once more and in just under forty minutes, the expected Air Iceland Fokker 50 took us back to a rainy and cold Reykjavik. Still, I returned to the hotel with a bright smile on my face. Sometimes, a lot can go wrong and the result still be great!

This was one of the magic little flying adventures that make our hobby so wonderful. What may look annoying at first sight — flight delayed, change of aircraft — turns everything into a whole new experience. Although the plan was to fly Norlandair's beautiful Twin Otter, what we got instead was even better: a flight on a Piper Chieftain, quite a difficult type to catch on scheduled flights these days, and some extra hours on what is a really sweet island: Grimsey. Had the flight operated as scheduled, we would never have met some of the island's lovely people, most notably the airport station manager / shopkeeper / church gardener.

Quite funny: a few weeks after the article was published, I received an e-mail from John Wegg, then-publisher of Airways Magazine. A reader from the US had sent him an e-mail with a picture of the station manager, holding the Airways magazine with my Grimsey article in her hands, bright smile in her face. Sometimes, articles like this one travel a long way and it made me very happy to see that it was so well-received on the island. Flying the Norlandair Twin Otter is still a dream of mine and would be a good reason to return to Grimsey one day.

TAAG — Angola's Flag Carrier

(appeared in Airliner World February 2014)

TAAG Angola Airlines is not only one of Africa's fastest growing airlines but also one of the continent's oldest. In a country that was paralysed by a terrible civil war for almost thirty years, keeping up its everyday operation or even surviving was not always easy for TAAG. In recent years, Angola has seen a phenomenal boom, fuelled, as so often, by huge oil reserves. Major investments have been made into the country's infrastructure and the country's national airline TAAG is making a big effort to become one of the top airlines on the African continent and has ambitious growth plans.

TAAG can trace its beginnings back to 1938 when Angola was still a Portuguese colony, and the airline was launched as DTA — Divisão dos Transportes Aéreos de Angola (this old name is where TAAG's IATA code DT stems from). Concentrating on domestic and some short regional routes, the airline's first aircraft were Dragon Rapide biplanes. The operation grew over the years and in 1948 the first DC-3s were added, as were the first Fokker 27s a few years later, with the route network ever-expanding.

Angola gained independence from Portugal in 1975 and the airline changed its name to Transportes Aéreos de Angola (TAAG). Angolan managers were appointed immediately after the country's independence and this was also when TAAG entered the jet age, receiving their first Boeing 737-200. The Boeing 737 was soon followed by a bigger Boeing 707-300 that allowed TAAG to launch its own flights to Portugal.

Tragically however, after gaining independence, Angola spiralled into a terrible civil war, which lasted for twenty-seven years and left the country devastated. Throughout the war, TAAG never stopped flying. If anything, the opposite was the case as a TAAG flight was often the only way to get around the country when roads were blocked or destroyed, and political violence made areas impassable. The airline also maintained vital links from Angola to the outside world.

Throughout the years, a very colourful mix of aircraft operated for TAAG, some of them leased for longer or shorter periods and many wearing the airline's stunning red-orange-and-white colours. Aircraft types included Yak-40s, L-100 Hercules, Ilyushin Il-62s, Lockheed L-1011-500 Tristars, Boeing 707s and Boeing 727-100s. In 1997, TAAG received its first of two Boeing 747-300s, purchased from Singapore Airlines. These newly-added aircraft allowed the airline to open new transatlantic routes to Rio de Janeiro and Sao Paulo in Brazil.

With the civil war finally over in 2002 and backed by huge oil revenues, Angola started to rebuild its destroyed infrastructure and also ordered new aircraft for its fully government-owned flag carrier TAAG. In a history-making event, TAAG took delivery of five brand new Boeing aircraft within just one hour on November 11, 2006: three Boeing 737-700s and two Boeing 777-200s. Both Boeing 777s were flown to Luanda nonstop from Seattle. With the introduction of these new aircraft, TAAG also planned the introduction of a new livery and some aircraft were even painted in the new scheme. Then, however, the company decided to stick to the old, more traditional colours that all of its aircraft still wear today, with the iconic Palanca (a giant black antelope), Angola's national symbol, painted on the aircraft tail.

TAAG's fleet has seen a major upgrade in recent years and today consists largely of modern Boeing aircraft. Five Boeing 737-700s (one of them a rare Quick Change version) are used on domestic and regional flights, with three Boeing 737-200s still complementing them on domestic routes for the foreseeable future. For longhaul services and busy African routes such as from Luanda to Johannesburg, a fleet of three Boeing 777-200s and two larger Boeing 777-300ERs have been acquired. The Boeing 777-300ERs are mostly used on the busy services to Lisbon. Three more Boeing 777-300ERs are on order and their deliveries scheduled for May 2014, December 2015 and March 2016. Once these aircraft arrive, TAAG plans to open new routes to Europe and potentially even to the United States where Houston would be the first destination (a busy route for the oil industry with very high yields). In Europe, Paris, London and Frankfurt would be the top choices for additional routes and the first of these may be opened early next year, once the first new Boeing 777-300ER is delivered to the airline.

As of now, Angola is a very regulated market, with limited

weekly frequencies that foreign airlines can operate. Although a number of airlines from Europe serve Luanda, limited frequencies result in very high yields. Portugal is a special case here. Angola was a Portuguese colony until 1975 and nowadays entertains good relations with Portugal. For decades, many Angolans went to Portugal to flee the country's civil war, looking for a better life in Europe. In recent years, with Portugal in a deep economic crisis and Angola's economy booming, this has been reversed and many highly qualified Portuguese come to Angola where they find well-paid jobs easily and speak the same language. The route from Luanda to Lisbon is the undisputed top performer in TAAG's network. The ten weekly flights are usually completely booked out, in spite of competition from Portugal's TAP, who also serve the route 10 times a week. In addition to Lisbon, TAAG also operates flights to Porto twice weekly and is quite happy with the route's performance. TAAG itself serves almost all countries in the Lusophone world, including two destinations in Brazil (Rio de Janeiro and Sao Paulo), two in Portugal (Lisbon and Porto) as well as the island of Sao Tomé, and Praia in the Cape Verde Islands.

The airline's international network reaches quite far into Asia — three weekly flights to Dubai (where cargo also plays a vital role) and a weekly service to Beijing. The vision of TAAG, according to Rui Carrera, is to serve all African capitals. Rui is member of the board of TAAG and vice-president for Flight Operations, Customer Services, Logistics, and Public Relations. As of now, he admits, the chances of achieving this may be rather remote. Yet the airline already offers flights to numerous African cities, including Cape Town and Johannesburg, Brazzaville in the Republic of Congo, Douala in Cameroon and Bangui in the Central African Republic. Neighbouring Namibia is quite popular with Angolans, as it offers visa-free entry for Angolan citizens, making the route to Windhoek one of the busiest for TAAG. TAAG's two longest routes are the flights to Beijing and Havana in Cuba. The route to Havana is a bit of a 'political' service — Angola has a shortage in medical staff and numerous Cuban doctors and nurses come to work in the country for a period of time. They make up the bulk of passengers on the service between Luanda and Havana, which operates only once a week (it used to be fortnightly only).

A look at TAAG's route map in the *Austral* inflight magazine reveals that codeshare agreements are in place with virtually all airlines that fly to Luanda. This is a prerequisite for most airlines serving Angola in order to be allowed to serve the country, rather than proof of real co-operation.

For domestic flights, fares are usually quite low and there are a number of competing airlines fighting for their share of the market. TAAG is mostly operating old Boeing 737-200s and, even with good load factors, finds it hard to break even on domestic routes. Inside Angola, the infrastructure is often still quite poor so flying is the quickest and safest option to travel from smaller cities to the capital city. TAAG serves fifteen domestic stations from Luanda; many of the routes are multi-stop flights as one destination alone could not fill a Boeing 737.

Speaking of the Boeing 737, currently the smallest aircraft in TAAG's fleet, Rui Carrera reveals that this aircraft type is indeed too big for many of TAAG's domestic and some regional routes. TAAG has started to look for smaller-sized aircraft types, including Bombardier's DH8-400 or Embraer's 145 and 170. No decision has been made so far but the introduction of smaller aircraft into the fleet is something that will happen in the near future.

2007 was a not a great year for TAAG. In spite of its brand new aircraft, the European Union banned the airline from flying to Europe that summer, citing safety concerns. This left the airline with a pair of Boeing 777s that were not allowed to fly to Europe — and not to Brazil, either, as they were not yet ETOPS-certified, a necessity for the long flight over water. While working on resolving the safety issues, TAAG at the same time opened new routes to Dubai and Beijing to keep its Boeing 777s busy and minimise losses.

For flights to Europe, the airline had to rely on (expensive) subchartered aircraft like a South African Boeing 747-400. In 2009, TAAG was given permission to re-start flights to one destination in Europe (Lisbon was an easy choice) using its own aircraft. Today, TAAG is allowed to serve all European countries once more, albeit restricted to its Boeing 777s and Boeing 737-700s. As Rui Carrera explains, the airline has improved internal procedures dramatically in recent years, and also passed the much-needed IOSA certification in 2009.

Luanda is in a very good location to serve as a hub for southern Africa and it is the airline's vision to develop its home base into a regional hub and as a connecting point for travellers between Latin America and Asia. When you draw a straight line between Beijing or Dubai and Sao Paulo, the detour to route via Luanda is minimal, making it a very suitable transit point. For flights from Europe to southern Africa, the same applies. On a flight from Europe to Namibia for example, Luanda would be much less time-consuming as a transit point than, say, Johannesburg, where quite some backtracking is necessary.

Until now it seems TAAG is taking very little advantage of Luanda's great location, and concentrating on point-to-point traffic. This may and will probably change once the new international airport becomes operational, already under construction some twenty-five miles (forty kilometres) outside the city centre and scheduled to open in 2015 or 2016. While some domestic flights may or may not (this has not been decided yet) stay at the present Quatro de Fevereiro Airport near the city centre, all international services will move to the new facility that will have a capacity for thirteen million passengers per year and twelve airbridges, something the present airport is also lacking.

The author sampled TAAG's services on two longhaul flights, from Lisbon to Luanda on a Boeing 777-300ER (in economy class) and from Luanda to Dubai on the smaller Boeing 777-200 (this time in business class). The evening flight from Lisbon to Luanda did not have a single empty seat, illustrating what an important market this is for TAAG. The cabin was impeccably tidy and very well-maintained. Throughout the flight, the cabin crew proved to be very safety-focussed, meticulously removing handluggage from emergency exits and checking that passengers were wearing their seatbelts and turning off electric appliances. Service was great, with good meals and a good variety of drinks available.

In business class, no flatbed seats are offered yet, but the current seats are comfortable enough for a seven or eight-hour flight from Lisbon to Luanda or Luanda to Dubai. In first class, TAAG offers flatbed seats that looked very tempting. While the inflight experience on TAAG was actually very pleasant, Luanda's airport and ground handling leaves a lot to be desired and this really spoils the whole experience. In the early morning hours, a number of flights from Europe arrived at the same time. The small arrivals building got so crowded that passengers had to wait outside on the apron, as the building simply could not take them all and immigration was extremely thorough. Having to wait outside for a while was actually not so bad, as temperatures outside were much lower than inside the building with it's underpowered air conditioning system.

Ground operations in general seemed a bit confused. After landing, it took half an hour until deboarding started. On departure, passengers were called to the departure gate more than one hour before departure and asked to board a waiting bus (there are no jetways at the airport). The full bus then waited for more than half an hour until it eventually departed to the waiting aircraft with no explanation given. In the evening, as numerous flights departed back to Europe and Dubai, the terminal was once more very crowded and could not cope with the number of travellers. TAAG's Welwitchia Lounge, accessible to business class and first class passengers, offered relief here and was a very pleasant place to spend a few hours before departure.

It is the goal of TAAG's CEO Pimentel Araújo to turn TAAG into a reference airline for Africa, complying with international standards in every regard. The experienced CEO looks back on a three-decade career in the aviation industry and seems like the right person to get TAAG to where its owner, the Angolan government, wants it to be. The temporary ban from European skies was definitely a wake-up call for the airline, as Rui Carrera explains, and the airline has since worked on its internal procedures to fully comply with international standards.

At the same time, the airline has improved customer service and its inflight product is in line with most of its international competitors, with lie-flat seats in First Class, individual IFE with a good variety of movies and music in all classes and very good inflight catering. A problem for TAAG is the substandard and often crowded airport in Luanda, something that will be overcome with the opening of the city's new international airport in 2015 or 2016.

Except for its Boeing 737-200s, which still ply the domestic skies and will be retired in the near future, TAAG's fleet is brand new.

In 2012, 1.2 million passengers were carried, a growth of fourteen percent over the previous year. For 2013, the airline expects a similar rate of growth. As Rui Carrera explains, TAAG expects to order more aircraft for a 2019 or 2020 delivery. But, should demand require this, he could imagine moving delivery of more new frames ahead. TAAG takes great pride in the improvements it has achieved in the past years. "We are looking forward to serving more European destinations, this time with state-of-the art equipment."

Another goal for TAAG are better financial results. At the moment, the airline is loss-making, much of it owing to the largest cost factor of every airline: jet fuel. Although Angola is an oil-rich country, jet fuel has to be refined abroad and imported, and the prices are among the highest in Africa (about twice the cost of fuel in Lisbon). Operating newer, more fuel efficient aircraft is one solution here and will also seal the fate of the remaining Boeing 737-200s sooner rather than later.

The impression of TAAG is that of an airline that has done its homework and improved both in terms of operation and product over recent years, yet is not reaching its potential. When developed properly, Luanda could become a very attractive regional hub and TAAG could benefit a lot from the city's strategic location and become for southern Africa what Kenya Airways or Ethiopian are for east Africa. With the airline now IOSA certified and effectively removed from the European blacklist, TAAG has done two important steps to become what CEO Pimentel Araújo wants it to be: a reference airline for Africa. It should be interesting to see how Angola's flag carrier develops in the years to come.

It was a dream of mine to write about TAAG for many years. Together with so many other airlines, I had them on my list forever, kept on writing e-mails, even letters in Portuguese, phoned and personally met their Berlin representative (who was a surviving relic from good old GDR times when TAAG flew to Schoenefeld). What I mostly got was: nothing, no reply whatsoever. Nevertheless, I kept on trying sporadically and one day, I could not believe my eyes.

After I contacted TAAG via their Facebook page, I received a message from their new PR lady, who spoke and wrote perfect English. Within just a few days, a visit to Luanda was approved and organised. A lovely evening in Lisbon had its perfect ending with a late night departure to Luanda onboard TAAG's fully-booked Boeing 777-300. In the morning, there was nobody meeting me and I ran around the entire airport for a good while trying to find Maria. Eventually, after some phone calls made by helpful airport staff of TAAG, she showed up at the airport and the rest of the day was a breeze. We even sat by a nice pool for lunch.

I took great pictures of TAAG's aircraft on the ramp, which is always the crucial part of producing a nice article. Interview cancelled? No problem. No pictures? Big problem! I walked around the airport ramp freely until I was red like a lobster from the sun. I almost met TAAG's CEO. As I was told, he is a bit shy. I saw him on several occasions during the day because the airline's headquarters are quite small. We stood very close to each other a number of times and still, were never introduced and he actively ignored me. That's fine. I got my pictures and enough friendly people talked to me and told me about TAAG's plans. After twelve very nice hours in Luanda (just about the right amount of time to spend there, so it seemed), I found myself on a TAAG plane back home, via Dubai, one happy man. It is definitely the article that holds the record for the longest wait to be realised. Who knows, maybe Surinam Airways, another airline I have had on my list for years, will break that record one day.

Nuuk Airport — Small Gateway to the Capital of Greenland
(appeared in Airports of the World November/December 2011)

Greenland is a large island and mostly white and not green, despite the name. For now, it remains an autonomous country within the Kingdom of Denmark. Just under 60,000 people live in Greenland permanently and settlements are small and far between. With no overland roads rom one town to the next to speak of, flying is the only logical way of getting from A to B here. In the 1970s, Greenland's Home Rule government decided to build a number of airports around the country to enhance links between the country's towns and settlements. Until then, the only airports of Greenland were the airbases or former airbases in Kangerlussuaq (also known by its Danish name Søndre Strømfjord), Narsarsuaq and Thule, all three able to handle big jets.

Nuuk, called Godthåb in Danish (hence the GOH IATA code) is the capital of Greenland and the biggest city by far, in fact the only one in Greenland deserving to be called a city. Being the capital, building an airport for Nuuk was a priority for the government. Around 15,000 people call Nuuk home. While this makes it one of the world's smallest capitals, it still is a quarter of Greenland's entire population. All of the island's government institutions are located here and the city has been growing at a fast pace for the last decades.

The new airport opened in 1979 on a hill just a few kilometres outside the centre. Like all the newly-built airports in Greenland, the facilities were designed for what would become the dominant aircraft in Greenland's skies back then (and still today), the four-engined de Havilland Dash-7. The airport's runway 5/23 measures a mere 3,117 feet (950 meters) in length. Due to the topography and the terrain surrounding the airport, lengthening the runway would be extremely difficult and although discussed in the recent past, the runway remains at its current length, sufficient to allow Dash-7s and the newer Dash-8s that Air Greenland acquired in 2010 to operate from here safely. Bigger aircraft, however, are totally out of the question and that is why Air Greenland's biggest hub remains at Kangerlussuaq, where the runway is much longer and the airline's Airbus A330 provides links to 'Mother Denmark'.

Before the airport opened in 1979, Nuuk was served by water planes landing in the city's harbour. After a crash of one of the PBY Catalinas in 1962, the airline acquired Sikorsky S-61 helicopters that could operate to most of Greenland's communities, carry twenty-five passengers more safely and reliably than the Catalinas and with very little infrastructure. The helicopters provided the only aerial links from Nuuk to the rest of Greenland for more than a decade. Interestingly, although now mostly operating on charters, the S-61 helicopters remain in operation with Air Greenland today.

On an average day, anywhere between three and up to ten passenger flights operate at Nuuk, all of them Dash-7s and Dash-8s. In addition, charter flights or cargo flights can be scheduled whenever the demand is there. Air Greenland's Dash-7s can be converted from all-passenger to combi or pure cargo configuration within minutes and often enough, passengers share the cabin with a load of cargo that can range from mail or fresh vegetables to sled dogs.

As Nuuk is also Air Greenland's major maintenance base, all of the airline's aircraft, with the exception of the Airbus A330, pass through Nuuk occasionally to undergo checks, including smaller aircraft like the Beech 200 (usually operating charters or air ambulance flights around Greenland) and helicopters. Most major overhauls are performed during the winter time, when a reduced number of flights operate.

All routes that Air Greenland currently flies from Nuuk are domestic, with the exception of a route to Keflavik Airport in Iceland that was launched in 2010 and is only flown during the summer months. The majority of Air Greenland's flights link the airport to Kangerlussuaq, where connections to Copenhagen and other places in Denmark can be made. Domestic destinations include smaller west coast towns like Paamiut, Sisimiut and Maniitsoq, the tourist draw of Ilullissat in Disco Bay, or to Kulusuk on the east coast. Most flights operate to more than one destination. Air Greenland is the only airline in Greenland offering domestic services.

Apart from the airline's red aircraft flying in and out, Air Iceland offers twice weekly flights to Nuuk from Reykjavik's downtown airport, using Dash 8-200s. Air Iceland is the only foreign airline serving the airport at the moment — Nuuk's short runway does not allow bigger aircraft from places further away to land here. The Air Iceland flights operate twice a week and do so late in the evening. As more and more passengers from Iceland or the rest of Europe choose to fly to Greenland via Reykjavik, the airline even decided to serve Nuuk on a year-round basis. In addition to passengers, this flight also carries fresh vegetables or dairy products to Nuuk.

In the past, flights did exist from Nuuk to Iqaluit in northern Canada. They were operated by First Air, in co-operation with Greenlandair (now Air Greenland), using Hs 748s of the Canadian airline and Dash 7s of Greenlandair. As of now, no direct link exists between the two countries but Air Greenland is apparently planning to resume services to Iqaluit using their new Dash 8s. This would cut the travel time down from at least two days to just around two hours.

The airport terminal is small and functional with a small area that can be used for international flights. The terminal has three gates and from all of them, passengers walk the short distance to the aircraft. Apart from the basics like check-in counters and a luggage belt, the terminal has a nice little cafeteria which is open whenever a flight departs or arrives and passengers are around. In the late morning, when Air Greenland's flights leave (sometimes up to three flights leave within an hour), the terminal gets very crowded. At other times of the day, it is completely deserted.

For the enthusiast, Nuuk is paradise. The only negative is the rather limited number of flights and the fact that there is only one airline operating the bulk of them. Nonetheless, behind the terminal, a hill rises above the airport. From here, beautiful pictures can be taken of aircraft on the ramp or on the runway. Everybody who has visited the airport will agree that a nice landing shot of an Air Greenland Dash-7 in their bright red colour scheme is something special. In addition to the hill behind the terminal, the low wooden fence surrounding the airport allows photographers to position themselves right next to the runway and get very close to arriving and departing aircraft. The terminal itself has a large front of glass windows which allows good views of the ramp and the two Air Greenland maintenance hangars.

When you have been outside in the often cold Greenland weather, you will be happy to spend some time inside with a hot coffee next to you. A few hours spent here will get you a good selection of Air Greenland's turboprop and helicopter fleet.

Nuuk's city centre is just three kilometres (around two miles) away from the airport. The city has been growing rapidly in recent years and the first houses are now much closer to the airport. From the elevated location of the airport, which sits on an artificial plateau above the city, great views can be enjoyed of Nuuk and the surrounding fjords. When flights arrive, there are usually a few taxis standing outside the terminal, waiting to take passengers into town. Apart from that, an hourly bus connects the airport to the city centre. And for more athletic visitors, it is also possible to walk into central Nuuk in less than an hour.

In 2008, the latest figure available, 63,575 passengers used Nuuk Airport and 4,032 movements were counted. With the addition of international flights to Iceland, this figure is bound to grow sharply and a resumption of services to Iqaluit would help, too. Nevertheless, because of its limited runway and unclear extension plans, operations from here will be limited to turboprop flights at least for the foreseeable future.

While downtown Nuuk with its many massive apartment blocks may not win a beauty contest, the old town with its small, colourful wooden houses is very scenic and the nature around Nuuk is stunningly beautiful. The city itself has some interesting museums such as the Greenland National Museum, which gives visitors a good idea of traditional Inuit life.

When I went to the Thai takeaway in central Nuuk to have the only affordable dinner in town, the Thai boy behind the counter (weird enough to see a Thai in Greenland) asked me, "Why you come here?" I answered, "Well, I'm a tourist. I wanted to see the place." His reply: "But is terrible!" It was hilarious and I couldn't say he was wrong. Nuuk as a city is pretty boring and ugly, much of it looks like a forgotten city in Russia and you meet a lot of dodgy people in the street. Still, I am very happy I went and enjoyed myself big time in and around Nuuk, mostly climbing on the rocks behind the little airport and taking pictures of Air Greenland's bright red Dash-7s and Dash-8s. The scenery around Nuuk is one of the most breathtaking I have seen anywhere and although it is expensive to come and stay here, it is money well spent. The article is another example of a story happening 'by accident'. No official interview or appointment, just many pictures taken at the airport and some research on the internet and still resulting in what readers hopefully thought was a nice article from a very special place.

Safi Airways
(appeared in Airliner World February 2009)

The name Safi crops up frequently in Afghanistan, as the Safi group of companies is part of a wide and diverse business empire. It all started when the wealthy Safi family, which has lived in exile in Dubai since the Soviet occupation of Afghanistan in 1978, began exporting palm oil back to its home country. More recently, the business group, now run by three brothers, has expanded into construction, import and export trading and even hotels — the Safi Landmark Hotel in Kabul opened its doors in September 2005. The latest Safi enterprise, Safi Airways, is perhaps the most challenging yet. Afghanistan has been in the daily headlines for more than seven years, and with ten million of the thirty million Afghans now living abroad, the chance to establish a scheduled service into Kabul was snapped up by Abdul Rahim Safi.

The carrier's first airliner, a second-hand Boeing 767-2J6ER, was acquired from Air China. After a major overhaul and repaint into its silver and blue Safi Airways' livery, the jet was delivered to the company's base at Dubai International Airport. Its inaugural service to Kabul was launched on November 17, 2007. Dubai is the perfect gateway for travellers, with non-stop flights to a rapidly growing number of worldwide destinations. With a constant stream of people wishing to travel between the two cities, it was a logical choice for Safi Airways' initial route. Such was its popularity; the frequency was quickly increased from five weekly rotations to a daily service.

Since its launch, the airline has operated a number of links combining Dubai and Kabul with other cities in the Gulf region, starting with a Dubai-Sharjah-Kabul rotation. However, the short hop to Sharjah proved too expensive, so flights were again centred on Dubai. Early in 2008, a lack of overnight parking space at Dubai International Airport forced Safi to ferry its jet to Fujairah, returning the following morning, ready for its scheduled departure to Kabul. In June 2008, it launched a Kuwait-Dubai-Kabul-Kuwait service, allowing both aircraft and crews to overnight in Kuwait City.

When I met Abdul Rahim Safi at the company's Dubai headquarters, I was fascinated by his future plans for the company and the development of Afghanistan. He compares the nation to a small baby, very fragile and exposed to any number of different influences, while needing other people's help to survive. Afghanistan, after decades of conflict, needs to 'learn to walk again' and is still dependent on other countries' support and advice. He believes that giving people jobs and the chance to earn money and lead a decent life reduces the chances of future conflict. One of his objectives in establishing Safi Airways is to create local jobs and generate economic growth. In the longer term, he sees Kabul as a transit point for international travellers flying between Asia and Europe.

The carrier currently has 180 employees, many of them westerners holding senior management and flight deck positions. As Abdul Rahim Safi explains, employing experienced professionals gives a start-up airline the best possible chance of success.

It operates from its headquarters in Dubai airport's free zone, where all its administration and planning is carried out. In Kabul, it occupies a large city office in one of the surprisingly flashy new buildings that are beginning to appear in the Afghan capital. Here, a number of reservation agents deal with enquiries made in person, by telephone or via the internet.

It continues to fly its single Boeing 767-2J6ER, YA-AQS (ex B-2554). The former Air China jet still retains its original cabin layout, with 18 Business Class seats and 196 in Economy. The airline regards itself as a full service carrier, with free meals and drinks for passengers travelling in both classes. International travellers make up a significant proportion of passengers, with many seats sold to military personnel, employees of security companies, diplomats, journalists and a growing number of business travellers.

Safi Airways is currently expecting the imminent delivery of two ex Air China B737-300s, following work by Indonesia-based GMF AeroAsia. In the interim, it has leased a B737-00 from Jordan Aviation. Once delivered, they will replace the B767 on the Dubai-Kabul service. The B767 will then start operating flights to Europe — initially to Paris via Kuwait, then to Frankfurt via Sharjah. The reason for the stops en route is not technical, but commercial — both countries have granted Safi Airways fifth freedom traffic rights, making the stop commercially viable.

Other destinations on the Safi Airways wishlist include a third European destination, London Gatwick, and connections to Delhi and Chennai. The carrier has already signed an agreement with Kingfisher Airways to provide onward connections for passengers inside India. It also hopes to establish a link to China, with Beijing the favoured destination.

According to Abdul Rahim Safi, the airline will grow its operation to five aircraft, with the addition of two further B767-200s, making Safi Airways' fleet the largest in Afghanistan. Apart from its international links, the domestic market offers further opportunities. As soon as the B737s are delivered, daily flights to Herat, in the west of the country, will be launched, to be followed later by a service to Kandahar. With roads outside the major Afghan cities often impassable and unsafe, flying is the logical alternative. There is great potential for a carrier to build a consolidated domestic network.

I travelled with Safi on one of its flights from Dubai to Kabul. My journey began at Dubai's Terminal 2, the current departure point for most links to Afghanistan, Iraq, and Pakistan, plus the occasional charter service. Our aircraft arrived from Kuwait on time, with a full load of passengers bound for Dubai and some connecting on to Kabul. As the Kuwait link was still relatively new, there was some confusion about the luggage of connecting passengers. The two legs are flown using two different flight numbers, but passengers' baggage had been labelled incorrectly with just one number. As a result, it all had to be offloaded and re-labelled, causing a one-hour delay. Pushing back at around 11.30, we quickly taxied to the departure runway and were soon on our way to Kabul. Our crew was truly international — the captain was Bolivian, the two first officers Canadian and American, and the cabin crew came from India, the Philippines and Malaysia!

The journey of less than two and a half hours took us across Iran and a corner of Pakistani airspace directly to Kabul. The cabin service was attentive, food and drinks excellent, and I was surprised by the high level of corporate branding visible throughout. As Abdul Rahim Safi explained, Safi regards itself as a full service airline and wants to offer an attractive in-flight product in both business and economy class, and the presence of the company's corporate identity is part of that strategy.

After a spectacular approach into Kabul, we arrived just forty-five minutes late. With a turn-around time of more than two hours, an on-time return to Dubai seemed eminently possible. Kabul's terminal is tiny and crowded, but a new facility is under construction next door. During my very brief visit, I was surprised by the amount of new construction and development taking place. It's not just at the airport that buildings are nearing completion, but in the city centre as well. There may be a long way to go before it develops into the hub for travellers that Abdul Rahim Safi envisions, yet some positive developments are already clearly visible. Who knows, he may yet prove all the sceptics wrong!

Almost seven years after my visit to Kabul, I am happy to state that Safi Airways is still around, something I would not have bet on when I visited the carrier. And not because of the airline's poor performance or management but simply because its home is Afghanistan, such a beautiful country yet such a mess. When I was invited to visit, I wasn't sure whether or not I should stay in Kabul overnight. But as everybody assured me it was 'quite safe' at the time, I went.

Safi Airways put me into the Safi Hotel in the city centre and adjacent to a very glitzy shopping mall. I felt brave and even walked around the block by myself and had a coffee at the Afghan version of Starbucks in the mall. Sat on the hotel roof and enjoyed the view of Kabul, probably the world's most dusty city. All good. Quite to my own surprise, I had no problem falling asleep that evening in Kabul. I thought I'd be more nervous. The next morning, I was told that I would be flying back to Dubai on Kam Air instead of Safi Airways, the other private airline in the country. Fantastic news for an airline collector. When we touched down in Dubai, I felt a bit of relief. And when the Safi Hotel got struck by a terrorist attack just a few months later, killing several people, it showed me that your time can be up any time and any place. I'm still very happy I went.

Flight to Khorog
(appeared in Airliner World October 2010)

When you have landed at St. Maarten, Kai Tak and Lukla, there is still one place in the world that a fearless air traveller should visit in his or her life: Khorog. The flight from the capital Dushanbe to this small mountain town in the Pamir mountains of Tajikistan is without doubt one of the world's most spectacular and exciting. The route, with about an hour of flying time, is operated by Tajik Air, the flag carrier of the central Asian country.

The flight to Khorog, scheduled daily, operates only in pristine weather conditions. This leaves me in doubt about our departure when driving out to Dushanbe's airport in the early morning, as the sky is cloud-covered. Although I have a number of spare days in case the flight does not leave on the first day, it would be perfect to have it "in the pocket" on day one.

Check-in takes place in the airport's small domestic terminal, adjacent to the small international terminal. With the assistance of a very helpful local guide, checking in for the flight takes a matter of minutes, although my flight ticket and passport go through the hands of at least five check-in agents, security officers, policemen and other persons involved in the process. No delay or cancellation is announced yet and the sky seems to clear up a little bit, maybe a lucky day after all?

Another domestic flight, to Khujand, is due to depart at the same time and around thirty passengers are waiting for their departure to be announced in the waiting lounge. The flight to Khorog is called first, putting a bright smile on my face, and just over ten passengers make their way to the bus waiting outside. A short drive across the vast apron of Dushanbe Airport (with a number of Tajik Air aircraft, including their splendid-looking Boeing 757, a Somon Air Boeing 737-800 and, surprisingly, a French Air Force Airbus A340 parked) brings us to the waiting Antonov An-28.

The An-28 is one of two aircraft types in the fleet of Tajik Air that can operate the route to Khorog and as most, if not all, Yakovlev Yak-40s have been retired from service, the An-28 is now the usual aircraft of choice. This rather unique aircraft with the double tail is boarded via a ladder to the rear of the aircraft. Passengers then climb through the luggage compartment into the passenger cabin and that includes a mother with her newborn child and an elderly lady, both of whom find it hard to get on board but are assisted by fellow travellers.

The last to board, as so often in the former Soviet Union, is the captain. He is in his fifties with a very red nose (and that is probably not because of inhaling the clear air in the Pamir mountains for years), but oh well. Everybody has taken a seat and we depart almost immediately. Unlike bigger aircraft types, the An-28 is allowed to start the engines on the parking position and then taxi out. (Bigger aircraft are pulled out by a pushback truck and only start their engines on the taxiway.) The same happens with arriving flights — engines are shut down on the taxiway and the aircraft pushed into its parking position. A rather odd procedure at an airport hardly handling twenty flights a day.

A very dynamic takeoff roll and seconds later we are on our way to Khorog. For the first half hour of the flight, nothing much happens. The landscape consists of green and brown rolling hills rather than mountains and one could almost get bored or put to sleep by the humming of the engines.

But then, after passing a crystal-blue reservoir fed by the Vaksh River, suddenly the mountains are there and you find yourself right in the middle of them. The Pamir mountains are some of the highest in the world. On our route, the highest mountains that we need to overfly measure up to 5,300 metres (17,389 feet) and the An-28's service ceiling is just above that when fully loaded. Five spectacular mountain ranges in short sequence and a little aircraft — that makes for an exciting continuation of our flight.

And indeed, the mountains get closer and closer and on some occasions, the Antonov seems to be flying through the eye of a needle, with steep mountain slopes to both sides of the aircraft and reaching high above where we are flying. On at least one occasion, I am convinced, snow is raised from a mountain top when we fly above it. The visible reactions of my fellow passengers reach from "I will just continue sleeping" to the very vivid discussions of two Austrian tourists of how close we really were to that last mountain range, followed by deep-drawn sighs when the next mountain has been safely passed.

Realistically, there were probably less than fifty metres between us and the nearest obstacle on a number of occasions.

In fact, much of the flight routes over Afghan territory. In the decades that the route between Khorog and Dushanbe has been operating, only one aircraft has been lost and it was not the aircraft's fault. In August 1993, during the civil war, a hijacked Tajik Air flight heavily overloaded with eighty-six passengers overran the runway at Khorog and crashed into the nearby Panj river. Only three passengers survived the crash. The pilots probably knew that this flight would never take off, yet with a gun pointed to their heads they did not have much choice but to overload the aircraft and try. This crash was the worst accident ever of a Yak-40, as the aircraft usually carries a much smaller number of passengers.

Our flight continues over hair-raising mountain crests and although they do not become any less frightening, by the time we start our descent, everybody on board has somehow got used to the thrill. Rather surprisingly, the landscape opens up and allows the little Antonov to descend down into the valley of the Panj river for the approach into Khorog Airport.

Khorog is a little mountain town with around 30,000 inhabitants. It is the capital of Tajikistan's autonomous region of Gorno-Badakhshan and has had a boost recently when the charitable Aga Khan Foundation decided to make the town home to one of three campuses of the University of Central Asia. Located in one of the poorest and most remote areas of the country, Khorog is a regional centre when it comes to things like administration, education or medical treatment. It is also an important market town for people from the region and also from Afghanistan, which is just across the river.

Khorog's main link to the outside world is the Pamir Highway. The term highway may be a bit misleading: traversing some of the world's most challenging terrain, the Pamir mountain range, the road is not even fully paved. The drive from Khorog to Dushanbe in a four-wheel drive may take anywhere from sixteen hours to a full day or longer, depending on weather and road conditions in this harsh region. When an avalanche or landslide has gone down, the link can easily be interrupted. Given the travel times and inconveniences of driving to or from Khorog, taking the flight of just over an hour is definitely a convenient, though thrilling, option and seats are in high demand both ways.

After landing, passengers just walk their way across the apron through a little gate to the street, where meeters and greeters are waiting patiently. To call it an airport terminal would be misleading. In fact, the actual building with the "Khorog" lettering on top does not fulfil any visible use at all. It is not used by arriving nor departing passengers, but it looks quite representative.

Apart from our little An-28, no other aircraft is to be seen and an airport official confirms that this is really the only operation taking place here. I am meant to return back to Dushanbe and am quite happy I have my confirmed ticket ready and handy, as demand for the flight is greater than the number of seats on offer. Reservations for the flight to Dushanbe are usually only accepted the evening before the flight. Then, when the flight cannot operate because of bad weather, passengers are moved to the next day. With an aircraft only seating eighteen, there seem to be far more passengers willing to travel with us.

The pilot enjoys a smoke during our turnaround and after a brief walk around the opulent airport facilities, it is time to check in for the return to Dushanbe. Check-in takes place in a separate little building, where passengers present their tickets and luggage which is then collected on one big heap. The Antonov has brought the return fuel, as no fuelling facilities exist in Khorog. Upon the captain's command, a "Da vai!" ("Let's go!") shouted across the apron, passengers walk to the aircraft and also carry their luggage along. A few minutes later, passengers and luggage, including two mothers carrying newborn children, a bucket full of apricots, a flight engineer sitting on a stool in the cabin and the captain are ready to go, almost. One passenger seems to be missing his seat. Turns out there are nineteen onboard instead of eighteen. The extra passenger does not hold a reservation, did not get one for today but decided to try anyways. The captain, rather annoyed now, sends the gentleman off the plane; we close the door and get ready for our return flight.

Somehow, when flying across the Pamir mountains, I had a better feeling with just eleven passengers onboard. Anyway, once more

I take comfort in the accident statistics. Our lift off is quite a bit less dynamic than on the way out, and once more pass over spectacular mountain tops, unbelievably close to some of them. The way the flight engineer is sitting on his bucket, scribbling in what seems to be his technical log book tells me to just relax and enjoy the scenery, some of the best you are ever going to get anywhere. A quick flight from Milan to Munich across the Alps on a clear day can be spectacular but this flight is a league of its own.

Just around three hours after our departure from there, we touch ground once more at Dushanbe. Nothing much has moved around the airport apron. A Tajik Air An-24 has arrived back from Khujand, the country's second biggest city. Discussions start as we have landed. Passengers feel that they should not be carrying their luggage to the terminal once more. The supervisor, on the other hand, feels that, indeed, they should. They load all their stuff (bucket full of apricots as one example) into the passenger bus, which then brings us to the brand-new 'Hall Of An Arrival', as the sign above the domestic arrivals area proudly explains.

This flight is definitely one of the most exciting ones you can do anywhere in the world. I strongly recommend to take it sooner rather than later as you never know how long it takes for a little airplane to be replaced by something more modern and powerful. Flight tickets on the route to Khorog only cost around €70 and can be booked through local travel agencies in Dushanbe. When doing a same-day return, no need to change sides for the return flight, both sides offer fantastic views.

The intention of many of my articles is to share beautiful flying experiences I've had while travelling. The flight to Khorog was on my list for many years and if I had to name the best flight I have ever taken in my life, it would be among the top three, if not in first place. Often enough, you travel far and wide to take that one particular flight and then, **** and ****, it just doesn't happen. Bad weather, aircraft broken or flying elsewhere, or even a coup? You name it. Anything can happen when you travel and that is why I was so amazed how easily I bagged the flight to Khorog. Fly to Dushanbe, nightstop in town, drive to the airport the next morning, fly to Khorog, fly straight back to Dushanbe (I would have liked to stay in Khorog actually) then spend the next couple of days just being lazy, driving around the capital and taking crazy pictures with the Tajik. Fantastic. Sometimes you have to be lucky. All of you will know stories very similar to this flying adventure. And when it works out: that's the magic of flying.

Finding a New Operator for Congo's Airports — and a Lot More...

(appeared in Airliner World January 2012)

The Republic of Congo (not to be confused with its much bigger neighbour, the Democratic Republic of Congo) is one of Africa's fastest-growing economies at the moment. At the same time, the country, following a short civil war in the late 1990s, still has very poor infrastructure. Upgrading roads, ports and airports has been a top priority for the Congolese government in recent years. Modern, functional airports are of course a lighthouse project for any nation and for many developing countries, increasing the standard of their airports is a top priority. Bringing in a partner with the necessary management knowledge through a concession is a way this is often done. In the Congo, the preparation of the strategy, the tendering process including the search for investors, and the negotiation of the concession agreement were completely managed with the support of Lufthansa Consulting, the German airline's consulting branch.

Hans-Dieter Janecke is a managing consultant at Lufthansa Consulting and has accompanied aviation projects on behalf of the company on all continents in the past decades. A fan of Africa, he decided to spend much of his time in the Congo during the last few years and has managed the concession project of the country's airports and a number of follow-up projects in the country. As he explains, the challenges during the tender process were numerous but some very positive results and improvements can now be seen.

When Lufthansa Consulting was first awarded the contract to privatise Congo's airports, one of the first tasks was to evaluate the different airports and get an overview. A team of consultants flew around the country in a chartered Cessna 404 to get an idea of the different airports. Congo's two main airports are at the capital city Brazzaville, and the port city of Pointe-Noire on Congo's short stretch of Atlantic coast. They were on the list, as was the airport of Ollombo in the country's north. Ollombo airport is very close to the birthplace of the president and developing the region is what could be called a presidential priority.

Eventually, these three airports were included in a tender inviting companies to hand in their offers. With Congo having very close links to France, both offers came from there. Eventually, on December 14, 2009, around three years after work on the project first started, the government signed a twenty-five year concession contract for the development, operation and maintenance of the airports in Brazzaville, Pointe-Noire and Ollombo with Aerco SA (Aéroports de la République du Congo) and Aerco associates SEGAP, a joint subsidiary of French company Egis-Avia and Marseille Airport, with the government of the Congo, and other Congolese private investors. Egis is very experienced in the field of airport management and is a shareholder in the consortium operating the airports of Larnaca and Paphos in Cyprus. Egis also manages the airports of Libreville in Gabon, Abidjan in the Cote d'Ivoire and Tahiti in French Polynesia through local subsidiaries.

The challenges, as one could imagine, are quite different from what you could expect at an airport of similar size in Europe or North America. To start with, airports are often unfenced. People by habit cross the runways, as do animals or even cars. At the airport in Pointe-Noire, people even have their little vegetable gardens on the airport perimeter. They were used to all that for decades and feel entitled to it, so telling them, "Sorry, you now have to take a long detour to get to the other side" is not an easy task. As Hans-Dieter Janecke remembers, in 2007, during one of his first visits, passengers were even picked up by taxis on the taxiway after landing. "This was actually quite convenient," he smiles.

Things have changed a bit now and will continue to do so, as Aerco brings the airports up to international standards. Having been awarded the concession contract in 2009, it took until April 2011 for the actual handover to take place from ANAC, the country's civil aviation authority and responsible entity for the operation of the airports.

Olivier Baric is the CEO of Aerco. When it comes to Pointe-Noire airport (PNR/FCPP), his main worry at the moment is apron space. Pointe-Noire is the economic powerhouse of the Congo. Oil companies and many international firms operate from here, while the administration is in Brazzaville. As many Congolese say, this is where the money is made. The airport inaugurated a new Chinese-built terminal in 2006 and the runway was extended to its current 2,600 meters (8,530 feet). Still, the apron is much too small to accommodate all airlines and aircraft that want to operate here. Pressure is particularly strong from the numerous domestic airlines who overnight their aircraft (mostly Boeing 737s) here.

As Olivier Baric explains, "Airlines suddenly start a new flight and the first we know about it is when the pilot reports to the tower when they are on approach. We then have to see how we can accommodate them here and with the small apron we have, this is very tricky." There are plans to pave a small parking area next to the existing one as a dedicated 'overnight apron' for the domestic airlines. Pointe-Noire is not only booming as a passenger airport (from Europe, Air France operates five weekly Airbus A330 flights to Paris and Lufthansa started serving the airport last November, using Privatair Boeing 737-800s) but also one of Africa's most important cargo hubs.

For years, a number of small airlines have operated a fleet of Antonov An-12s on cargo flights to the Capital Brazzaville. Pointe-Noire is vital for the provision of the country's hinterland with food, equipment and whatever you can imagine. The main road between the coast and Brazzaville is not yet fully paved, thus not usable during the rainy period. The Congo River is not navigable all the way between the Atlantic coast and the Capital Brazzaville, thus flying is essential. When an An-12 operated by Trans Air Congo crashed on approach to Pointe-Noire in March 2011, all Antonov flights were halted. Most of these aircraft now rest at the airport in Pointe-Noire and wait for whatever the future holds for them.

This, however, increases the pressure for apron space and they were simply parked on an unpaved area next to the runway. At the moment, two Ilyushin Il-76s fly back and forth between Pointe-Noire and Brazzaville. They can, however, carry much less cargo than is needed and it will be interesting to see what solution will be found once the rainy period arrives. The airport's terminal is way too small at peak hours and not in the best condition, although only a few years old. A new terminal structure will be constructed in the near future, but, as Olivier Baric explains, "Without more apron space, we can build as many terminals as we want, it will not solve the problem."

One of the challenges of operating here is also that there are often conflicting interests. At Pointe-Noire, a number of nice villas have been built very close to the runway, too close to comply with ICAO regulations. The homeowners, who received their right of abode from ANAC, the country's aviation authority, now have a feeling of entitlement and cannot easily be convinced that their houses need to be removed to comply with international aviation regulations. Although the Congolese government wants its airports to comply with international standards, local interests often interfere with these plans, leading to delays in construction and whatever other projects.

Another handicap for the new operator are passenger figures that have not been very reliable in the past, especially on domestic flights. This is now a thing of the past. At Brazzaville airport, boarding passes of all passengers are being scanned. At Pointe-Noire, where such technology is not yet available, an airport representative now counts all passengers boarding an aircraft to ensure the airline's figures and the airport's figures match.

At the Maya-Maya Airport in Brazzaville, progress is more visible. The airport has a brand-new terminal, commissioned at the time of the handover of the airports to Aerco in April 2011. A new glass building with all the bells and whistles of a modern airport — three airbridges, air conditioning, modern luggage carrousels — the terminal is a quantum leap over the previous structure, a tiny building without air conditioning (and virtually without anything) that burst at the seams whenever an Air France A330 arrived from Europe. The new terminal will be mirrored, with the extension already visible. Upon completion of the second half of the building, one portion will be used for domestic flights (about two thirds of the passengers in Brazzaville are domestic), one for international flights.

Brazzaville also received a second, parallel runway measuring 3,300 x 45 meters (10,827 x 148 feet) which will be inaugurated shortly and complement the existing single runway. As in Pointe-Noire, apron space is an issue here, but during the author's visit the pavement of an additional area was currently underway.

With the privatisation of the airports and the handover to

Aerco to operate them, work was not over for Lufthansa Consulting. As Hans-Dieter Janecke explains, follow-up projects are always of particular interest to the company. "You know the country and the environment you are working in, you know the decision makers. It is a lot easier to work on a follow-up project than to acquire an entirely new project somewhere else."

In the Congo, Lufthansa Consulting had been awarded the job to create a masterplan for the development of the three main airports. In 2010, work began on the conception of an 'Airport City' (called Maya-Maya Village) at the airport in Brazzaville, additional infrastructure including a commercial centre, a conference venue and an airport hotel.

Another interesting project, also assisted by the consulting team from Germany, is the launch of a new national airline, Equatorial Congo Airlines. The airline was to receive its first aircraft, a Boeing 737-300, in September 2011 and intends to start operations on the busy Pointe-Noire to Brazzaville route. For the new airline, Lufthansa Consulting developed a five year business plan, including future routes and fleet. They will also oversee the adherence to international quality and safety standards, something that cannot be seen as a given in a country that as a whole is on the EU blacklist.

The third airport in the concession contract is in Ollombo, in the Congo's north. The country's president Denis Sassou Nguesso was born in the area and it was a personal priority for him to include Ollombo's airport in the concession deal. Work at the airport is already at a very advanced stage, with a brand new 16,000 square metre (172,222 square feet) passenger terminal (a building that Pointe-Noire's airport would be happy to have probably) and a 3,000 metre (9,843 feet) runway. At the same time, the region is not yet fully developed and there is no public electricity line to the airport yet, the whole structure running on generator power.

At the moment, no scheduled airlines fly to Ollombo. This may, however change in the nearer future with a number of airlines having the airport, probably the best equipped one in the country for now, on their radar. Once more, Hans-Dieter Janecke is one of the people trying to come up with ideas for how to develop this airport, now that it exists, to a sensible use. One of the ideas is the creation of a training centre for airline crews here, but nothing has been decided so far.

As can be seen, obstacles during the concession process and in the everyday operation of an airport here are manifold, and patience is the vital quality of the consultants working on projects. Nonetheless, "At the end of the day," Hans-Dieter Janecke explains, "It is very rewarding to see how progress, even at a small pace, is made and the Congo's airports brought up to international standards."

This was a very interesting little trip that Lufthansa Consulting helped me realise. We are all used to (and expect) shiny and modern airports no matter where in the world our travels take us. It often takes years and decades to plan and actually build them, not only in Germany, which is famed for its efficiency and the capability of its engineers (laughter from the Berliners in the audience). The story of the three airports in Congo (one of them is hardly used at all and seems more like the president's toy) and their privatisation is truly a very positive story in many ways. The airport in Brazzaville in particular has come a long way and is one of the most pleasant airports on the continent. The small Republic of the Congo, unlike its much bigger troubled neighbour, the Democratic Republic of the Congo, is a very peaceful and civilised place, at least for the time being. Hans-Dieter, the consultant who accompanied me during my visit and told me everything about this project, has become a good friend.

Eznis Airways

(appeared in Airliner World November 2011)

Mongolia is a vast and sparsely populated country squeezed between its two neighbours, Russia and China. It has a population of only 2.75 million citizens, and almost half of them today live in the capital Ulaan Bator. Driven by a boom largely based on its huge mineral resources, Mongolia will be one of the world's fastest growing economies in the years to come.

In a booming country with long distances and poor roads between cities, air travel is growing at a fast rate too. One of the main beneficiaries of this development is the country's youngest airline: Eznis Airways (airline codes: ZY/EZA).

The name 'Eznis' may sound strange at first but is easy to explain: EZ simply stands for 'easy' and 'nis' is Mongolian for the verb 'to fly', so the pronunciation is actually similar to 'Easynis'. Founded only in 2006, Eznis today carries most domestic passengers in Mongolia, and has strong international ambitions. Munkhsukh Sukhbaatar, the airline's young CEO, only joined the company last year. When meeting him at headquarters in downtown Ulaan Bator, he seems enthusiastic about the airline's achievements so far, and things to come.

"When you look for challenges that an airline could face, Mongolia really has them all," he explains. "Mongolia's climate can be very hot in the summer and very cold in the winter. It is one of the highest countries in the world. We have a very sparse population and cities are far between, even by plane. Ground infrastructure is often very basic — some of the airports we fly to do not have paved runways and can be very dusty places. Regulations are in many cases still developing and being brought up to international standards. So it is really very challenging to set up and maintain a reliable and very safe operation."

Yet, Eznis Airways has been on the sunny side for most of its existence. At the time that it started flying (its inaugural flight went from Ulaanbaatar to the city of Choibalsan in eastern Mongolia in December 2006), MIAT, Mongolia's government-owned airline, was having many issues with its own domestic flights and the fleet of

Antonov An-24s had reached the end of their operational life. The Mongolian government then decided to leave the domestic market to private airlines and let MIAT concentrate on international flying. The idea behind this was to allow the small private airlines (at that time, Aero Mongolia was the dominant domestic carrier and Eznis had just entered the arena) to develop undisturbed and let MIAT ensure service on the core international routes to European and Asian destinations.

The aircraft of choice for Eznis was the Saab 340B. This type can accommodate thirty-four passengers and has sufficient range to serve all domestic routes from Ulaan Bator. Together with the manufacturer, the aircraft saw some upgrades like the installation of a gravel kit, a powerful heating system for the cold Mongolian winters and the newest Enhanced Ground Proximity Warning System (EGPWS). Today, five years later, Eznis operates four Saab 340s on a busy domestic schedule linking fourteen domestic and two international destinations to Ulaan Bator.

In June 2011, Eznis received its first-ever jet, an Avro RJ85. The aircraft previously flew with Lufthansa Cityline as D-AVRD, and at the end of it's tenure there underwent a complete overhaul that included the installation of a brand-new cabin interior. CEO Munkhsukh Sukh-baatar explains why this aircraft was chosen: "While the Avro has relatively high operating costs, it seemed the right aircraft to us because the acquisition costs were quite low, the size of it is right for our busier routes and it has the capability to operated from gravel runways, which is a must-have for us, as some of the airports we fly to do not have paved runways." This is especially true for some of the airfields used for mining charters, an increasingly important business for Eznis. The newly-opened mines are mostly located in the southern part of Mongolia, close to or in the Gobi Desert. The airport facilities there are less than basic, with gravel runways being the norm and no landing aids whatsoever.

Still, the RJ85 can perfectly operate in and out of there, as David Wiggins, a British captain 'on loan' to Eznis, explains. He is training local pilots converting from the Saab to the Avro and was delighted by the performance of the Avro on these very basic runways during some test flights.

Mining charters are an essential contributor to Eznis revenue. With new mines starting their operation all the time, mine workers are usually transferred back and forth every couple of weeks as they go to work or on leave. The intervals they spend at the mine are longer in the summer. To rotate workers in and out, this means more mining charters in the wintertime for Eznis.

This perfectly coincides with the very seasonal demand for air travel in Mongolia. Many Eznis passengers are tourists visiting this beautiful country. And while more and more tourists come to Mongolia each year, they usually do so during the short summer season, when demand peaks for just around three months. Thus, in the warm time of the year, the Eznis fleet is busy with its regular schedules while in the winter, additional demand by the mining companies makes up for less demand on scheduled flights and keeps the fleet busy.

A second Avro RJ85 will have joined Eznis as this article goes to press and Munkhsukh Sukhbaatar reveals that the airline is looking at additional routes outside Mongolia, with all significant destinations inside the country part of the network now. "Northern China could be interesting and we are also analysing cities in Russia and Kazakhstan."

Traffic rights with neighbouring countries are such that one airline of each country can serve a certain route but not more than one. This means that core routes like to Beijing or Seoul are currently out of reach for Eznis, as they are already served by one Mongolian (MIAT) and one foreign carrier (Air China and Korean Air respectively). Thus, the airline must look at secondary markets.

It already serves two international routes at the moment: Ulan-Ude, a big Russian city with a strong Mongolian influence located just east of Lake Baikal is served three times a week, and Hailar in northern China which sees flights from Ulaan Bator with an intermediate stop in Choibalsan, a city in eastern Mongolia. Apart from the second Avroliner, Eznis does not plan any further aircraft acquisitions at the moment. As Munkhsukh explains: "We need to prove the business case for those two first of all. We are thinking about additional jets, maybe even freighters, but we want to give it some time and see how the present two integrate into our operations."

The Avros, purchased from Lufthansa Cityline, are maintained by Lufthansa Technik crews from Switzerland. With the growing fleet, Eznis is also currently building its first own hangar at Chingis Khaan Airport in Ulaan Bator, due to open in December 2011. Previously, maintenance was either done under the blue Mongolian skies or in one of the other airline's hangars at the airport.

CEO Munkhsukh Sukhbaatar admits even he was surprised by the rapid growth of the Mongolian economy and the demand in air travel. 2010 saw roughly fifty percent growth in the domestic demand for air travel. Mining charters have seen 260% growth over the previous year. These explosive growth rates of course also have to do with the low base they started from, yet are much higher than anticipated by anybody and bound to continue in a similar way in the coming years.

Some interesting figures that illustrate how small the domestic market still is and how much potential growth can be expected: in 1990, the year that saw the collapse of the Soviet Union and most of its allies, around 900,000 passengers took a domestic flight in Mongolia. In the following years, the economy collapsed and so did domestic flying. In December 2006, when Eznis started flying, things were starting to get better slowly and ever since, growth rates have been positive. Still, last year, only around 150,000 passengers were counted on the domestic flights of all airlines.

Flying often seems without an alternative here. Travelling by car from Ulaan Bator (located in the middle of the country) to a city like Khovd in western Mongolia can easily take up to three days, a distance of 1425 kilometers (885 miles) along bad roads or pistes. In summer this is still doable, but in winter not only do travel times increase significantly but driving is becomes outright dangerous at times. Considering the alternative, a flight of just under two hours in the Avroliner, the choice seems easy. Yet, not too many Mongolians travel by air frequently, as buses are much cheaper and travel times are not such a big issue.

In May 2011, Eznis signed a co-operation agreement with All Nippon Airways, covering arenas such as management and operations. Already, a Japanese Chief Operations Officer has been seconded to Ulaan Bator. Having an engineering background, Mr Hiroshi Kitahara's main task at the moment is to take the company through IOSA certification, due to take place next year. The IOSA certificate is a minimum requirement to enter codeshare or any other co-operation agreements with most airlines these days and when receiving it, this will open the door for Eznis to become more of an international airline.

The co-operation seems beneficial for both parties, with ANA gaining a foothold in what may become a very interesting market in the future, and a small airline like Eznis having one of Asia's leading airlines as a partner will help broaden its activities and expand its operation.

It seems logical that both airlines will set up a flight between Japan and Mongolia soon, with no Japanese airline currently serving the country, and such plans do exist for the near future. Whether or not ANA is to purchase a stake in Eznis seems undecided at the moment but is not ruled out entirely. As of now, Eznis is fully owned by its founder, the Newcom Group, one of Mongolia's leading investment companies.

The author travelled on two Eznis domestic routes: a flight to Murun, a busy tourist destination in one of the most picturesque parts of the country on the Saab 340; and a triangle flight from Ulaan Bator to Ulaangom and Khovd, two important cities in the western region of Mongolia, on the new Avroliner. Both flights were almost fully booked, early August being the peak summer season in Mongolia.

The flights underlined the impression of a very profession-ally-run airline. Departures were on time and the interiors were in immaculate condition. Eznis attaches great importance to little details — while other airlines would just operate aircraft the way they received them from the previous operator, Eznis installed a new cabin interior on both the Saabs and also the Avroliner. The Eznis logo, an orange flower, is ever-present, be it on the wrapping paper of the inflight meal, a very tasty meat pie, on the coffee cup, or the airline's own inflight magazine.

The flight attendants are very professional, speak excellent English, and provide passengers with a truly friendly and efficient service on all flights. When infrastructure on the ground is often so basic (the check-in counter at the small airport of Murun consisted of a wooden table, a laptop and a printer), the Eznis inflight product is perfectly on a par with any regional airline around the world.

There is probably little reason for the airline not to be optimistic. Mongolia is one of the world's fastest growing economies, and demand to travel to and around it will continue growing at a fast pace. After five years of flying, Eznis has a very efficient and stable operation up and running, and the integration of the Avroliners seems to run very smoothly too. The airline hopes for the signing of open skies agreements between Mongolia and its neighbouring countries, which fuel the airline's growth opportunities even more. Even when acting rather conservatively, Eznis will become a much bigger airline than it is now and possibly become a more important regional player in this part of the world.

Mongolia was one of the countries I always wanted to visit. And when I finally went, Eznis was one of the airlines that I arranged a visit with. And what a cool airline they were! Everybody from CEO to flight attendant to ground staff seemed to be in a 'Yes we can' kind of mood and this seemed to be true for the entire country. Construction was everywhere as Mongolia was trying to reinvent itself and become a modern country. I loved every bit of my visit to Mongolia, some of the sweetest, most open-minded and welcoming people I have ever met.

However, soon after this visit, Mongolia's economy took a dive when the prices for minerals dropped sharply and demand for domestic travel plummeted. Eznis tried to shrink its operation for some time, got rid of its jets (they had even operated a Boeing 737 for a while), and in the end operated only a small fleet of Saab 340s and DH8-400s. Yet, once more a well-run airline fell victim to an economic crisis and probably to its own ambitions also. Eznis, so it seems, wanted too much in too little time and maybe this is true for Mongolia as well.

To Sochi by "86"

(appeared in Airways March 2011)

The 350-seat Ilyushin Il-86 is — together with its successor, the Il-96 — the only wide-body passenger aircraft produced in the Soviet Union, although a combination of limited range and poor economics ensured that it never became an export success. Nonetheless it provided important people-moving capacity on the trunk routes of Aeroflot in the 80s and a myriad of Russian independent airlines in the 90s.

Today, only a dozen of the 106 Il-86s built remain active. Outside Russia, most countries have banned the type for non-compliance with noise regulations, the two exceptions being Turkey and Egypt, both popular with Russian tourists. The principal commercial operator of the Il-86 is Atlant-Soyuz Airlines (IATA: 7B ICAO: MOA), which was renamed Moscow Airline last September. Based at Moscow-Vnukovo International Airport (VKO), it proudly markets itself as the 'Airline of the Moscow Government'.

During the northern summer months, the route between Moscow and Sochi — a Black Sea resort in Krasnodar Krai, and the city hosting the 2014 Winter Olympics — is one of the busiest in Russia. Tourists from practically everywhere in Russia flock to Sochi. This demand is reason enough for the Il-86, which is normally assigned to charter work, to be pressed onto scheduled flights.

A few weeks after obtaining confirmation of my booking — so far it has been the best £99 ($165) I ever spent on an air ticket — I checked in at Vnukovo. Ambitious as plans for Vnukovo's development may be, it was not a pleasant experience because air conditioning was either out of service or not working properly. Besides drinking over-priced coffee there are few retail distractions, and the main entertainment is airplane watching (photography is prohibited).

Flight 7B 201 to Sochi was scheduled for 15:50 local time, but it was about an hour late. Even though the Il-86 was parked at an airbridge, we were bused to the aircraft and boarded using three integral airstairs in the belly of the plane. Coming up the wide stairs from the lower deck into the cabin, you feel as though you have boarded a cruise ship. Flight attendants gave directions to our seats. The flight was not full, with only about 200 passengers onboard, and within a few minutes we were leaving on our journey to the Russian Riviera.

After taxiing out to runway two-four — the slightly shorter of the two intersecting runways — and waiting for three landing aircraft, we positioned for an immediate and very noisy takeoff.

The climb rate could be described as pedestrian — even worse than that of a fully loaded Airbus A340 on a hot day. On what was effectively a two-hour sector, the aircraft never really seemed to reach cruising altitude. About half an hour into the flight, drinks were served (although the two gentlemen sitting next to me had already downed a couple of whiskeys from their own bottle by then), followed by a snack accompanied by tea and coffee. After a flying time of around one hour and forty minutes, we started our descent, and the four Kuznetsov NK-86 twin-spool turbofans enjoyed a bit of respite for the first time since we departed from Vnukovo. Touchdown on runway zero-six at Adler-Sochi (AER) was two hours and four minutes after takeoff, and the thrust reversers made what Neil Diamond would have called 'a beautiful noise'.

We parked at a remote stand and were again bused to the terminal. The airport's newly completed terminal building offers a pleasant environment, although baggage delivery was bewildering, with passengers sent back and forth as flight numbers displayed at the carousels kept changing over the next hour. An irritation for most, no doubt, but this writer still basked in the experience of flying by Eighty-Six to Sochi.

PLUNA - the Rebirth of Uruguay's Flag Carrier
(appeared in Airliner World November 2008)

One of the oldest carriers in Latin America, PLUNA (Primeras Líneas Uruguayas de Navegación Aérea) is the national airline of tiny Uruguay. Founded as early as 1936, PLUNA has made it through a number of ups and downs during its history (although, especially impressive given the hostile terrain and weather of the region and unlike nearly all of its South American competitors, this airline has never had a fatal accident).

Its first routes were domestic flights from Montevideo to the cities of Salto and Paysandu in the north of the country, operated by a pair of five-seater de Havilland Dragonflies. In 1951, PLUNA was nationalised. It experienced further growth, both in terms of network and fleet and was one of Latin America's first airlines to receive jets. During the airline's heyday, the network included cities like New York and Miami. The only other intercontinental destination is Madrid, while the routes to the USA have long been closed. For decades, both PLUNA's network and fleet only changed slightly. The only Boeing 707 was replaced by a DC-10, and a younger Boeing 737-300 joined the older -200s. A single Boeing 757 and an ATR42 joined the fleet. What was lacking was a real concept — and a plan to make the airline profitable.

In 2007, seventy-five percent of PLUNA were purchased by Leadgate Investment, a private consortium of investors from Germany, the USA, Argentina and Uruguay. Before that takeover, PLUNA had been re-nationalised by the Uruguayan government following the collapse of Brazil's flag carrier VARIG, up to that time a major shareholder in PLUNA.

Matías Campiani, one of the investors of Leadgate, is now PLUNA's CEO. This job is his first in the aviation industry so far and quite a challenging one, as he admits. Interestingly, David Bonderman, a major stakeholder in Ryanair, is one of the co-investors in the new PLUNA. While in the short time since takeover and privatisation, many changes have taken place inside the airline, it has also become most obvious to the outside world that some major changes are being implemented. The most striking one is PLUNA's new corporate identity which had its premiere on the fuselage of their first brand-new Canadair RJ900s.

And indeed it seems as though a breath of fresh air has started blowing in Uruguayan aviation since. The PLUNA just before the recent privatisation almost completely resembled the PLUNA of fifteen or twenty years ago. The airline has been flying on almost exactly the same network: the bread-and-butter air bridge between Montevideo and Buenos Aires' Aeroparque airport, regional flights to Santiago de Chile, Sao Paulo, and the oceanic route to Madrid. Additionally, holidaymakers were flown from Argentina to the Uruguayan beach resort of Punta del Este, and Uruguayans to beaches in Brazil.

Even the airline's aircraft fleet had not changed a lot in the last twenty years: four Boeing 737-200s forming the backbone. This is all going to change — quickly! By early 2009, the Boeing 737s will have left PLUNA's fleet, even the sole newer -300 series.

The same applies to the Boeing 757, an aircraft that PLUNA never really had a suiting route for except for the occasional holiday charters or… the Hajj! In 2007, the Boeing 757 and a number of crews was leased out to Med-View Airlines from Nigeria, operating Hajj flights from a number of Nigerian cities to Saudi Arabia. Nice extra business for the airline and an exciting time for the crews involved, as Matías Campiani explains with a smile. So in a year's time, PLUNA's fleet will consist of two aircraft types: seven Canadair 900s and a Boeing 767-300 flying the route to Madrid.

Some streamlining in the network has taken place already. The Madrid route, previously operating with an en-route stop in Rio de Janeiro, is now flown non-stop, enabling PLUNA to offer four weekly roundtrips instead of three. Of course, such a long and long-standing route bestows a lot of prestige upon such a small airline. That said, if prestige is the only benefit from such a route, the airline's survival might be in doubt one day. In 2007, the Madrid route was a major handbrake on PLUNA's finances and thus, improvements here are crucial to the airline's well-being. Since changing the route to a non-stop operation, results have already improved, both in terms of load factor and yield, but the route is still in the red.

Here comes Montevideo's new role as a hub airport, which will significantly change the way the airline operates and also contribute to the success of the airline's only long-haul route. While quite conveniently located between the economic centres of Argentina and Brazil, PLUNA had never really taken much advantage of the location of its home base — most of its traffic was point-to-point. Uruguay with only 3.3 million inhabitants is a very small market and the potential for new routes is of course limited. A number of regional services to neighbouring countries failed simply because of the size of the Uruguayan market. With a functioning hub system, this problem can be solved, as a number of airlines have shown, such as KLM and Emirates.

More or less from day one it was obvious to the new owners that with an elderly fleet, an efficient and profitable hub operation attracting new travellers seemed unlikely. New aircraft were needed and ideally that would be an aircraft type with just under 100 seats and low trip costs. Of course affordable acquisition costs and a quick delivery were two additional prerequisites.

Only two aircraft manufacturers seemed to offer what PLUNA was looking for: Embraer and Bombardier. With the Embraer production line effectively booked solid for years, PLUNA would have had to wait for quite some time before the delivery of the first Embraer jet. Bombardier was able to offer delivery of the first Canadair RJ900 within a year. Also, as the first customer of the type in South America, it is not hard to guess that the incentives offered to PLUNA by Bombardier will have been quite significant.

The first CRJ900 was delivered to PLUNA in late March 2008. CEO Matías Campiani and a number of PLUNA employees travelled to Bombardier's Montreal plant to accept the new aircraft and take it home, a delivery flight which routed via the Turks and Caicos Islands and Manaus in Brazil.

According to Campiani, the new Canadairs are the ideal aircraft to operate on the existing regional network of PLUNA and explore new markets. The new aircraft are operated in an all-economy ninety seat configuration. Business class on short haul flights will be a thing of the past, along with a number of frills. On regional flights, PLUNA aims to bring fares down while offering a number of services for sale rather than 'on the house'. Food on board and priority boarding will still be available — for a charge.

Compared to the Boeing 737s, the Canadairs mean a significant capacity cut. Where the capacity is needed, such as on the routes to Buenos Aires or Sao Paulo, additional frequencies have been added already or will be in the future. The relatively low operating costs of the Canadair RJ900 will allow PLUNA to explore new markets while keeping the financial risks of failing on a new route controllable. A radius of 1500 to 2000 km around Montevideo encompasses much more than just the metropolises of Buenos Aires, Sao Paulo and Rio de Janeiro.

A number of lesser-known cities that still boast a large population significant industries yet lacking connections by air are waiting to be discovered. PLUNA has identified a number of such ports, analysing population and industries there, and connecting links where demand can be expected. An example: the cities of Curitiba in southern Brazil and Cordoba in Argentina (in fact Argentina's second-biggest city) are both home to a number of car manufacturers or affiliated industries, a reason to assume there might be interest from business travellers for a swift connection between both cities

Travelling on one of the legacy carriers like VARIG, Aerolineas Argentinas or TAM, a possible itinerary could look like this: fly from Cordoba to Buenos Aires (Aeroparque). Take a cab to Buenos Aires' international airport Ezeiza. Fly to Sao Paulo (Guarulhos). Take a cab once more to Congonhas airport. Fly to Curitiba. A long day! This example is a typical situation for travellers not going from one big hub to another, and a market PLUNA wants to capitalise on. Until now, Brazilian low-cost airline GOL is the only carrier starting to explore the region's smaller cities and create convenient links.

When travelling between much of Argentina and Brazil, a stop in Montevideo is not a big detour. Offering a connecting time of around an hour and reasonable prices would make the product quite attractive for potential passengers. The hub concept has already started to some extent, making use of the existing routes in PLUNA's network. Schedules of the Montevideo-Madrid flight and those of regional routes have been harmonised to allow connections from Cordoba and

Buenos Aires (Aeroparque) as well as Santiago de Chile. At the other end, co-operation agreements have been signed with Spanair and other European carriers for connections beyond Madrid. In Montevideo, PLUNA now offers regional connections for passengers arriving on American Airlines from Miami. In the near future, PLUNA is striving for further co-operation with more carriers — besides offering its own connections via Montevideo, the carrier aims to be a feeder and distributor for other airlines where it makes sense commercially.

When landing at Montevideo's Carrasco airport, one thing is quite obvious: the place is small and quite pleasant, but old and definitely not built to be a modern hub. With just one airbridge, most passengers travel to and from the terminal by bus. However, what passengers can also see is a new terminal under construction, a very modern and airy structure. The timing could be any better for PLUNA and probably for the airport as well. In early 2009, just around the time PLUNA expects delivery of their seventh Canadair CRJ900 (the last one on order for now, an additional eight are on option), the new terminal will become operational, offering much-improved facilities for travellers and airlines alike. Carrasco Airport was privatised in 2003; since then, improvements have been made on the existing terminal and the main runway extended to 3,200 metres, enough to allow for non-stop intercontinental departures, which were limited under certain conditions before.

Matías Campiani seems very optimistic about PLUNA's future (even if, as a CEO, that is part of his job). However, given the current economic upturn in the region, a brand-new fleet of Canadair 900s arriving and the new terminal opening just in time, there are a number of indications that PLUNA's ambitious plans might indeed become a reality fairly soon.

Uruguay has always had a special place in my heart since I went to school there for a few months. My host father was a pilot for PLUNA, the national airline of a country with about as many inhabitants as Berlin. When I went to school there in the 1990s, PLUNA flew a single Boeing 707 as far as Madrid, plus a fleet of Boeing 737s, and just introduced a DC-10, which unfortunately subbed for the Boeing 707 on my flight back to Europe after my time there. I always followed PLUNA more closely than any other Latin American airline, so when the opportunity arose to visit them for an article and write about their privatisation, I went. Unfortunately, their plans did not work out and PLUNA was liquidated in 2012, leaving Uruguay without its own airline. When I visited Montevideo Airport in 2013, most of their fleet was still parked there. A privatisation gone wrong.

Around the Block and Back with New England Airlines

(appeared in Airways February 2012)

Not many will have heard of a small airline called New England Airlines. For the inhabitants and visitors of Block Island, the airline makes a huge difference. Islanders and tourists make good of use of what is a very reliable connection between the island and the coast of Rhode Island in the northeastern USA in even the most severe weather conditions.

Block Island is by no means a big island, measuring just 9.7 square miles (25.2 square km). It is located in the Atlantic Ocean, approximately thirteen miles (twenty-one kilometres) off the coast of Rhode Island, and about the same distance away from the eastern tip of Long Island. Just over 1,000 people live there permanently. This number greatly increases during the busy summer months, when the climate is perfect and many New Englanders set up their summer residence there or come for vacation.

While ferries from the mainland do exist, the quickest way to reach Block Island is by plane. Since 1970, New England Airlines has been providing an aerial link to the island from the small airport near Westerly, Rhode Island. And it has never gone beyond that, apart from the charter flights it offers, always staying the little airline it was when founded in 1970.

Westerly is the airline's home airport and its entire fleet of three Islanders (including some of the oldest built), three Piper PA-32s and a single Piper PA-28 are based there. Westerly is located almost exactly halfway between New York and Boston and can be reached easily by car or train. The flight to Block Island, usually operated by one of the airline's three Britten-Norman Islanders, takes around ten minutes, sometimes less.

The airports at both ends are small and uncongested, there are no security checks, and passengers can easily arrive fifteen minutes before departure. Another plus is that flights can still operate when ferries are confined to port in bad weather.

Block Island's small airport (BID / KBID) was opened in 1950 and recently received a brand new passenger terminal, inaugurated in

2009. Its single runway 10/28 measures a mere 2502 x 100 feet (763 x 30 meters), which is perfectly sufficient for Islanders and smaller aircraft to operate from. At the other end of the island, Westerly State Airport (WST / KWST) is a bit bigger and a bit older. In the 1920s, Westerly began with a grass runway. During World War II, it became a navy base, the runways were paved and the airport expanded. The airport has two intersecting runways, 7/25 and 14/32. Runway 7/25 measures 4010 x 100 feet (1222 x 30 meters) and 14/32 almost the same at 3960 x 75 feet (1207 x 23 meters). Westerly has a small and modern airport terminal with free parking at the doorstep. Both Block Island and Westerly airports are operated by the Rhode Island Airport Corporation.

During a visit to the area last November, despite the appalling weather, I decide to treat myself to a quick flight to Block Island and back, just for the fun of it. A quick drive from the Interstate 95, Westerly State Airport can be reached within minutes from the small downtown area or virtually all the towns in the vicinity. Buying a ticket takes a minute and my request to return with the same flight and not stay on the island does not even raise an eyebrow. It seems like some other enthusiasts have done it before. "We're fine with it, as long as you pay for it!" is all the check-in agent has to say.

The next flight is just thirty minutes later, time to have a look around the small airport's hangars and the perfect views of the apron and its inhabitants. The terminal is very convenient and more than sufficient for the short time passengers spend here. A great plus these days is that no security screening is necessary for passengers because the aircraft are so small.

Just five minutes before our scheduled departure, the pilot himself calls passengers to board the aircraft, one of New England Airlines' Britten-Norman Islanders, registered N404WB. He helps with the boarding, loads passengers luggage and some groceries.

Groceries? Yes, the airline co-operates with the Shaw's super-market in Westerly and also a local pharmacy. Islanders can order their groceries by phone or fax and they are delivered from the supermarket to the nearby airport and flown to Block Island where people can then pick them up. Extremely convenient for people living on the island and additional revenue for airline and supermarket.

Today, just five passengers fly over to Block Island. The pilot (this is a single-crew operation) warns us the flight will be rather bumpy and this is not an empty promise. Flying at just over 2,000 feet, the little Islander is shaken back and forth by gusting winds, accompanied by heavy rain. On what is a grey November day, it is hard to imagine how beautiful this area must be in the summer.

Just eight minutes after take-off, the pilot artfully touches down on runway 10 of Block Island's small airport. After a short taxi we park in front of the airport's new passenger terminal. The building, constructed in the style of maritime architecture you often see around New England, has a small check-in counter and a cafeteria and once more offers good views of the apron. Some meeters-and-greeters pick up passengers, one of whom has undergone surgery on the mainland. Two locals have come to pick up their shopping bags from the flight.

Things are rather quiet today; once more there are only five passengers on the return flight to Westerly. After around ten minutes on the ground, the pilot calls passengers to board the return flight to Westerly, flight number EJ 401 (yes, New England Airlines even has an IATA code).

Once more, the flight is rather turbulent but my fellow passengers seem to be frequent fliers on the route and do not mind at all. For them, the flights of New England Airlines mean more reliability when travelling to the mainland. On this particular day, the ferries had to stop sailing because of the weather conditions, while the flights were still operating routinely. A roundtrip costs eighty-four US dollars for adults and commuters can get significant discounts on the fare.

Flights leave hourly in both directions, with departures half past every hour from the mainland and on the hour from Block Island. During the busy summer months, additional flights are scheduled when there is demand. And while New England Airlines' scheduled operation is limited to the route between Westerly and Block Island, the airline offers charter flights across the continental US (and even to Timbuktu on their website). Most of the time, charter flights would operate to airports in the region and not only to and from Block Island or Westerly.

For anybody visiting the area, I would recommend this little trip. It can easily be done in an hour or two while you are passing by. Flying on New England Airlines is a bit like flying in the good old times before low cost carriers, super-thorough security checks and the like. Service is very personal and it your flight will be a memorable experience. And if you do have the extra time, Block Island seems to be not only a very exclusive but also a very beautiful little island.

Are you male? I guess most readers here are. Do you have a wife or girlfriend? She's not overly interested in aviation? Sounds familiar to me. When on vacation together, sometimes you have to play little tricks to fly a particular aircraft or visit an airport missing from your logbook. "Oh, is there really only that one flight with all the stopovers? No direct flight?" I am sure most of our wives and girlfriends completely understand what's going on but they play the game and play dumb just because they love us avgeeks so much.

When I was a little kid, I used to play Microsoft's flight simulator. That was in the early 1990s and graphics were not even close to what we have today. You basically flew through patches of green (land) and blue (sky or water) and suddenly, there was a runway that looked like it was taken from Super Mario. While Chicago's Meigs Field was always my favourite (and the standard departure airport when launching the simulator), another airport I often flew my Cessna 182 from was Block Island. A tiny little island off the New England coast. And while I never managed to fly from Meigs Field in real life before it was shut down overnight, a vacation trip to New England suddenly put Block Island back on the agenda after I had completely forgotten about it. I did a little research and found out that an airline was actually offering scheduled flights there: New England Airlines, a tiny airline with a very basic website reminiscent of the time when I was 'flying' to Block Island as a kid in the nineties.

On our drive from Connecticut to Rhode Island, purely by coincidence of course, the road took us past the little airfield of Westerly, where flights to Block Island depart. I parked the car, went into the small terminal and asked if I could do a quick roundtrip to Block Island. No problem. Cool. The lady of the house, although I offered to pay her roundtrip fare, preferred to stay in the car and read her book and didn't mind me doing my little flight if it made me happy. That's true love! So off I went on New England Airlines' little Islander into skies laden with heavy rain and strong winds. It was nice to see Block Island in 3D for the first time, although the visibility was quite poor. It would be nice to come back on a sunny day. When I asked the Captain if I could take one of the safety cards with me and he said "Sure, I know where to find them," that really made this one-hour trip perfect.

Little adventures like this one are really what the magic of flying is all about for me. If I were to choose between a longhaul flight in First Class and a flight on New England Airlines to Block Island on a rainy and stormy day, I'd go for the Islander flight. Easy decision.

Saba Airport
(appeared in Airports Of The World September / October 2011)

When you ask somebody interested in aviation if he or she has ever been to the Caribbean and the answer is yes, well, then they have probably been to St. Maarten, one of the most spectacular airport-beach combinations in the world. And while St. Maarten is a fantastic place to spend a few days, one of the island's small neighbours deserves an equal share of fame, for its airport and the island itself: Saba. Saba Island, today a 'Special Municipality' of the Netherlands, is just over ten minutes flying time from the hustle and bustle of St. Maarten, yet seems light years away. It is much less crowded, seems greener and lusher, and the relaxed locals seem to have their own pace. Unspoiled is definitely a good word to describe the island and that is also what Saba calls itself: 'The Unspoiled Queen'.

Winair, the airline based at Princess Juliana Airport in St. Maarten, operates five daily Twin Otter flights here and the Twin Otter is about the only aircraft that can land on Saba and carry a significant number of passengers (together with Britten-Norman Islanders and probably the Dornier 228). With just 1,300 feet (396 meters) in length, the single runway 12/30 is probably the shortest runway of any commercial airport in the world and definitely leaves no room for an aborted take-off or a late landing.

Located on a plateau, called Flat Point, the airport is flanked by steep hills to one side and steep cliffs at both ends of the runway. When coming from St. Maarten, passengers sitting on the left hand side of the aircraft or behind the pilot (there is no cockpit door on the Twin Otter) can already see the airport a few minutes before touchdown. It is nestling on the island's only plateau, when the rest is just steep slopes. Just before landing, the Twin Otters perform a left turn to get on the extended centreline, then steeply dives down and touches the runway asphalt on the first few metres — nothing short of spectacular!

The airport's small terminal is painted in white and green, the dominant colours on the island, most houses also painted in the same colours. With just five Twin Otters landing here every day, the terminal is small and functional, not much bigger than the airport's impressive firetruck. It has a small coffee bar, a nice place to celebrate your arrival and make plans for your time on the island or kill time before your departure.

From the airport, one of the lowest points on the islands, a winding road leads uphill and to the island's two main villages, Windwardside and The Bottom. As the road is the only major one on the island, it is simply referred to as 'The Road'.

The airport's history really began in 1959. That was when Rémy de Haenen became the first pilot ever to land on Saba, on what was just a provisional runway, on a flight from the neighbouring island of St. Barthelemy. By doing so, he proved all the skeptics wrong who said that an airport could not be built on the island. The current airport was opened a few years later, in 1963. It is named Juancho E. Yrausquin Airport after the minister of finance who assured the financing of the airport when it was built. Ever since, a limited number of scheduled and non-scheduled flights have operated to Saba.

Today, Winair is the only scheduled operator to what is strictly speaking an airport closed to commercial traffic, marked by an X on each end of the runway. Operating to Saba is only allowed to those carriers obtaining a waiver from the local authorities. Winair is the only airline providing scheduled services to the neighbouring island of St. Eustasius and to their 'hub' in St. Maarten — a lifeline for Saba's approximately 1,700 inhabitants and a convenient link for visitors. Flights to St. Eustasius are usually operated in a triangle or with a stopover en route to or from St. Maarten.

In addition to these scheduled flights, occasional charter flights are operated by Winair or Anguilla Air Services, the latter using Britten-Norman Islanders. The small airport apron, which also has a designated helicopter landing pad, is just south of the runway with taxi times of just a few seconds usually and when a Twin Otter has landed, it seems about full. The small terminal has just enough room for a single check-in counter, a small inside waiting area and some office rooms. The main passenger waiting area is outside, just in front of the aircraft. For those with more time, a small snack bar, called The Flight Deck, offers snacks and beverages.

The airport's control tower only offers advisory services, not full air traffic control. Aircraft fuel is not available on the island, which is not a problem as the flights are very short and aircraft often fly many rotations with the same load of fuel. After landing and taxiing to the apron, the Twin Otters usually leave one engine running while passengers disembark and luggage is being unloaded. Turnaround times between flights are just a few minutes.

Although Saba Airport, because of its topography and occasional strong winds, has a reputation of being one of the most risky airports in the world, no accidents have ever happened here — perhaps such a marginal field concentrates the mind? For anyone in the area, I would strongly suggest a visit to Saba, even if it is only for a few hours or even for a few minutes, to experience the spectacular landing and take-off. The island has a surprisingly large number of attractions on offer to visitors, be it a climb up Mt. Scenery, the island's highest peak (and the highest peak of the Netherlands by the way), snorkelling and diving, or simply enjoying the laid-back life on the islands. Several visitors have even decided to take up residence and live here permanently.

I could spend the rest of my life flying in and out of Saba. Have a little coffee or small bite to eat at the bar in the cute terminal and enjoy the feeling of remoteness that you have here although Saba is just over ten minutes flying away from crowded St. Maarten. I am sure every flight would be different and special and I am sure I would be one happy man.

Arik Air

(appeared in Airliner World October 2009)

Until now, Nigerian airlines were not famous for reliable and safe flight operations, attentive customer service or a particularly long life. All this seems to be bound to change. Arik Air is one of the newest airlines in Nigeria and what it has achieved in its less than three years of existence is truly remarkable.

The story starts with a disappointed entrepreneur. Sir Johnson Arumemi-Ikhide holds a variety of interests in the energy, construction, agriculture and food sectors in Nigeria. One day, he was on his way to sign a contract in the Nigerian capital city of Abuja. However, his flight ran late (nothing really unheard of in Nigeria) and the planned deal fell through.

Alas flying is really without alternative in Nigeria. Roads are in poor condition, a rail network practically non-existent, and it can take days to get from A to B, depending on the weather. So for whoever can afford it, flying has to be the logical choice. Even before this unlucky event, Sir Arumemi-Ikhide had spent years travelling around the country without ever being able to rely on air transportation — this day was an eye opener for him. In 2002, the flag carrier Nigeria Airways was going through severe problems and eventual liquidation at that time, so he purchased his own Hawker 850XP Business Jet.

This private transport was initially only meant to take him around the country on his business travels safely and on time. However, word got around quickly and soon many of his business partners and friends wanted to use the business jet instead of the unreliable local airlines. It was then that Mr Arumemi-Ikhide not only decided to purchase a second Hawker Jet but also to set up something that seemed to be in high demand: a Nigerian airline that operated reliably and efficiently with a high level of customer service.

Arik Air was born, although it was still a while before operations were launched. The name Arik is an abbreviation of Sir Johnson's family name, Arumemi-Ikhide. He started looking for the 'right people' to start the new venture, knowing that he could benefit from international expertise when the goal was to create an airline truly superior to the other carriers operating in Nigeria.

In April 2006, Arik Air took over the former Nigeria Airways facilities at Murtala Mohammed Airport in Lagos, which were in devastating shape. A number of old aircraft were decaying on the apron and needed to be dismantled, the hangar and administrative buildings were in severe need not only of a pot of paint but much love and care.

While it would have been easier to build a new structure, Arik Air's chairman is passionate about history and wanted to keep the old Nigeria Airways buildings, the 'cradle of Nigerian aviation'. Major reconstruction work and a huge clearing-up operation started immediately and only a few months later with a 'new' hangar in place for them, in October 2006, Arik Air took delivery of its first aircraft, three brand new Canadair CRJ 900s. Two Boeing 737-300s were also accepted by the airline before the launch of operations.

On 16 October 2006, the Nigeria Civil Aviation Authority granted an AOC to Arik Air and the inaugural flight took off just two weeks later, on 30 October. Initially, flights were operated on what is called the Golden Triangle, between the capital Abuja, centre of the country's administration, the commercial capital Lagos, and resource-rich Port Harcourt in the Niger Delta, where most of the oil and gas resources of Nigeria are to be found. For the first few months, Arik Air's operation was domestic only.

It was and remains the airline's goal to pick up market share in the domestic market, then start regional operations, and last but not least go intercontinental. Throughout 2007, new aircraft were delivered, including the airline's first Boeing 737-700NGs, another Canadair CRJ 900, three smaller CRJ 200s, and two Dash 8-300 operated by Dutch ACMI specialist Denim Air on behalf of Arik. The turboprops operate on a new route to Port Harcourt's City Airport, a Nigerian Air Force Base that Arik Air helped develop into a commercial airport that has become very popular with passengers for its proximity to the city centre (Garden City Terminal, as Arik Air calls it, only allows turboprop operations because of its short runway). New destinations like the city of Kano in northern Nigeria, or the lesser-known Jos, Warri, Benin and Enugu, soon joined the network.

Just a few months after the launch of operations, in early 2008,

Arik opened its first regional route, from Lagos to the Ghanaian capital Accra, just forty minutes away by air.

In April 2008, Arik received the approval of the US Department of Transport to start direct flights to the United States which clearly underlines the airline's bold ambitions, as do the aircraft that Arik has on order.

Another milestone in Arik Air's short history was the inauguration of flights to London. A pair of Airbus A340-500s became available when Kingfisher Airlines did not have any use for them. When the chance arose, Arik Air gladly took the two aircraft to start long haul flights a little earlier than anticipated. The two A340-500s are operated by Portuguese airline HiFly although Arik Air flight attendants make up more than half of the cabin crew.

The London route is one heavily travelled by both Nigerians living in the UK and visiting their families at home (or vice versa), and by business passengers. Before Arik Air started flying the route, four airlines had served before them. Two of them were Nigerian: Bellview Air and Virgin Nigeria (who stopped all longhaul flights in the meantime) and two from the UK: Virgin Atlantic and British Airways. According to Arik Air, the route was frequently oversubscribed and passengers were offered relatively poor service for high fares. When entering this market, as on shorter flights Arik Air wanted to offer a product superior to any of the competition.

A big plus for Arik Air is the connectivity at the Nigerian end. Passengers can book a through-ticket from London to all domestic points. International passengers arriving to Lagos are assisted by Arik Air and offered a shuttle bus to the domestic terminal for their connection, so in spite of the less-than-perfect airport infrastructure, the connection process is made as smooth as possible for them.

Michael McTighe is Arik Air's managing director and previously worked with Britannia in the UK and Ryanair in Germany. It is exciting to listen to the stories that the Scotsman has to tell about the previous two years in Africa. A major obstacle for any airline is financing, and being a Nigerian airline does not make things easier when it comes to receiving financing from banks or other lenders. This is why Arik has been fastidious about paying back all money due perfectly on time.

Many Nigerians, including the media, could not believe what they saw when they first flew with Arik Air: brand new aircraft (it had been more than twenty years since a Nigerian airline took delivery of a factory-fresh aircraft) and a very high and consistent level of operational reliability and customer service. A number of prejudices about Nigerian airlines in general had to be overcome, as McTighe explains. According to him, it has paid off to put in place a strong team of experts, for example relying on the maintenance services of Lufthansa City Line, who take care of the fleet of Canadair jets in Lagos, or an international management team in combination with local knowledge, an important combination of experience.

Often enough, the managers from abroad tend to be surprised to discover quite how unique the Nigerian market really is and that something that was a success in Europe can not necessarily be copied one to one to the Nigerian market. As an example, Nigerian passengers mostly buy their ticket on the spot, which means they come to the airport some hours before the flight, have a look around the different counters for possible offers, buy whatever flight looks convenient, and in more than ninety percent of cases, pay cash. This makes it very difficult for an airline to plan ahead.

And it illustrates why low-cost airlines as we know them would probably not work in Nigeria, as passengers are just not used to buying a ticket months before they travel. For any airline operating in Nigeria, a number of obstacles remain. The airport in Lagos, the country's major gateway, is in need of improvement, and many of the country's smaller airports have only seen minor repairs, if at all, since they were constructed in the 1970s or 1980s. Besides infrastructure, weather often causes delays. Besides the frequent heavy thunderstorm, poor visibility often delays flights as many of the Nigerian airports are VFR-only. Last but not least, and quite ironic in an oil-rich country like Nigeria, a lack of fuel is another circumstance that can cause delays, particularly so at the country's smaller airports.

As of summer 2009, Arik Air operates a fleet of twenty-seven aircraft, most of them delivered new from the manufacturer. It is the largest commercial airline in Nigeria and holds a forty-two per cent market share in the domestic arena, where it connects twenty-two destinations via its two hubs in Lagos and Abuja.

Regionally, Arik Air flies to Accra in Ghana, Banjul in The Gambia, Dakar in Senegal, Freetown in Sierra Leone and Cotonou in Benin, with further expansion due as new aircraft are delivered. The launch of daily flights from Lagos to Johannesburg will be followed by further long-haul flights later this year.

By May 2009, two and a half million passengers had travelled on Arik Air. The airline's first Boeing 737-800, 5N-MJN, just recently delivered to the airline, is the first aircraft truly custom-made for Arik. It has sixteen seats in business class and 136 seats in a quite generous layout in economy, with all seats featuring individual IFE screens.

For other aircraft, the airline took up delivery slots of other airlines with the cabin interior already in place. The CRJ 900s were not taken up by Air Canada Jazz and feature their generous seventy-four seat configuration. Of the Boeing 737-700s, two were 'inherited' from low-cost airline SkyEurope with an all-economy 149 seating configuration, while the other frames (previously ordered by Air Tran) have business class seating and a more generous 12/119 seat configuration. The all-economy version of the Boeing 737-700 operates on routes to northern Nigeria, where there is very little demand for a business class.

As of now, the superstars of Arik Air's fleet are the two Airbus A340-500s it operates on its routes to London Heathrow, and to Johannesburg. They were not taken up by Kingfisher Airlines and feature the airline's truly superior cabin interior with an impressive bar in Premier Class where passengers can while away the flight and have a drink, IFE in every seat and a seat pitch of thirty-four inches in economy class. The inflight service is second to none in both classes.

Arik Air wants to reach the highest service levels of international carriers yet offer a Nigerian touch as well. This shows in the cabin crew of course, most of whom are Nigerian. You can have typical Nigerian food like a hot pepper soup or chicken stew. You don't fancy that? Well, then you can have a Greek salad or a European main course instead.

'Nollywood' movies are shown in both classes and are hugely popular with Nigerian passengers. As a matter of fact, the Nigerian film industry is the world's third-largest today, behind the US and India. So a number of small yet important elements have been considered that make both Nigerian and international passengers feel at home on Arik Air's flights.

Behind the scenes, Arik Air has invested heavily in employee training at international standards and also at maintaining the high level of operational responsibility it has achieved. To date, twenty-five employees have benefitted from a Boeing Corporation Airline Planning Program, six underwent Canada's Bombardier Management Program and six pilots were sponsored on Air Traffic Pilots License training in the US. Another sixteen staff, ten engineers and six flight dispatchers attended specialised courses. At the inception of its operations in 2006, Arik Air instituted a scholarship program aimed at training Nigerian graduates to become pilots.

A state-of-the-art Operations Control Centre has been completed at the airline's Lagos headquarters that allows the airline to monitor the weather conditions and locate its aircraft wherever and whenever they are flying or on the ground. While Lagos is Arik's main airport for all international flights, Abuja as a second hub plays an important role for the domestic operations and will also see international flights in the future. As of now, Arik Air plans the construction of a major MRO facility in co-operation with international partners and the location for the new facility may well be Abuja, as the airport is much less congested and offers unlimited space, unlike Lagos.

As of now, no such facility for heavy maintenance is available in West Africa — aircraft have to perform intercontinental ferry flights for overhaul, either to Europe or South Africa. From day one, Arik Air has trained local employees and set up the Arik Air Academy that trains technicians, ground staff, as well as future cockpit crews. It is clearly Arik's goal to not only deliver attractive returns for the airline's investors but also leave a long-lasting positive impact, for example by training locals for highly-qualified jobs.

The airline currently holds orders for seventeen more Boeing 737-800s and -900s for deliveries up to 2014, two Bombardier Q400s, three more Canadair CRJ900NGs due in 2009. It is one of the few customers of the passenger version of the Boeing 747-8 Intercontinental, with four on order for delivery in 2014. Five Boeing 777-300ERs are due between now and 2011, and seven Boeing 787-900s in 2013/14. With the current rate of expansion, it does not at all seem unlikely that earlier delivery slots from other companies may be sought, or that interim aircraft will be leased to allow for the opening of new routes.

So what does the future hold for Arik Air? What the airline has achieved so far is tremendous. In less than three years, it has established an impressive network, a stable operation, and extremely high level of service. Many smaller things are still on the agenda, like the launch of a frequent flyer programme or a dedicated inflight magazine. With more long haul aircraft on order, direct flights to the United States will happen sooner rather than later, with more international destinations to follow suit.

The network around West Africa will be significantly expanded and it is Arik's aim to serve all capitals around the region. On the domestic side, more destination cities will be opened, many of which have never seen scheduled air traffic before. Interestingly, two years ago nobody would have bet on Arik Air's success, but the general opinion seems to have turned around. Media coverage in Nigeria and abroad is very positive, Arik Air has won a number of awards (such as the prestigious International Quality Summit Award) and passenger numbers are growing fast. A number of neighbouring countries currently without an own airline now turn to Arik Air for their expertise. In fact, Arik Air has been awarded national carrier status in both Niger and Sierra Leone. It seems that so far, this young airline has done everything right — it is likely that Arik Air will become the dominant airline in West Africa. And, finally, an airline that Nigerians can take pride in!

Soon after this article got published, I got a very angry letter from a reader. He was accusing me (and his tone was quite rude) of painting a very rosy picture of the airline and asked how much they paid me to write this 'advertisement' for them. We stopped the short-lived conversation pretty quickly as I could not convince the gentleman that I did not receive any money from the airline to write a positive article about them. I went through the article again and compared to what I'd seen during a short visit to Lagos. And had I had to write the article again, it would have stayed pretty much the same. Some parts of the world are really hard or special to do business in and Nigeria is one of them for sure, for a number of reasons. And what the Arik Air team achieved within a very short time was truly remarkable. They built a very stable operation and an excellent product, not only by African but by international standards. And Arik is still around today.

Flight to Antarctica by Ilyushin Il-76

(appeared in Air International September 2010)

Antarctica, one of our planet's seven continents, is often imagined as a massive frozen landmass without any infrastructure, hard to get to, and as hostile as a place can be. This may be true for most of Antarctica. Yet, in the last few years, interest in Antarctica has grown and a number of airports are now operational on the continent. These mostly consist of an ice runway and are only open for the southern summer — basically early December until early February. This is the time when most scientists, construction workers, official visitors and tourists flock to Antarctica.

One such airport is Novo Runway, close to and named after Russia's Novo Lazarevskaya station. Located in the protected Schirmacher Oasis, the station is about five and a half hours flying time by jet in a southwesterly direction from Cape Town in South Africa. Cape Town, the city closest to this station, has been used as a gateway for ships travelling to Antarctica for years.

In 2001, Antarctic Logistics Centre International, specialising in polar shipping and aviation transport for the Russian Antarctic Mission, set up a regular air bridge between Cape Town and Novo Station to cater for increased demand for travel to and from Antarctica. For all visitors, the rather short flight results in much higher efficiency compared to a boat trip several days long. The time previously spent travelling by ship can now be used for research projects and / or construction work on location. A significant gain, as the southern summer, the time during which travel to and from Antarctica is possible at all, is very short as it is.

Novo Airbase, as most people call it for short, is located at 70°50'S and 11°35'E. Its southern location, 70° south, would be the equivalent of the northern tip of Norway, central Greenland or northern Alaska in the northern hemisphere. While the actual station is located in the protected oasis near the coastline, the airport is about 400 metres (1,312 feet) higher, on a flat ice plateau, about fourteen kilometres away from the station. In terms of flying time from Cape Town, Novo Airbase is one of the most accessible points in Antarctica, the prime reason why it was chosen not only as a gateway to Antarctica but also as a distribution point for connecting flights.

Connecting flights? Indeed! The airport is only one of several runways served as part of the so-called DROMLAN Air Network. DROMLAN is an abbreviation for Dronning Maud Land Air Network. Dronning Maud Land (Queen Maud Land in English) is the part of Antarctica closest to Southern Africa. The network was established in order to establish an aerial link between Cape Town and Novo Airbase and further beyond to a number of stations in Antarctica. Eleven nations, all of which run their own scientific programmes on this part of the continent and rely on the transportation of their scientists and equipment, are involved in DROMLAN and finance it.

When it was launched in 2002, Novo Airbase was the only runway capable of accepting an Ilyushin Il-76. Since then, a second facility has been built and upgraded, the Norwegian Troll station, to the west of Novo Airbase and a bit further inland.

Most of the flight operations are run by the Antarctic Logistic Centre International (ALCI) as the official aircraft operator of the Russian Antarctic expedition. Not an airline itself, ALCI leases the aircraft and crews from other companies. In the past summer season, the Il-76 was provided by Transaviaexport from Belarus while the Basler BT-67s (stretched and reengined turboprop DC-3s) were operated by Kenn Borek Air from Canada. In addition to the flights provided by ALCI, the national research institutions sometimes operate their own aircraft such as the BT-67 operated by the German Alfred Wegener Institute. In order to achieve the highest level of efficiency, schedules are co-ordinated between the different operators.

Novo Airbase consists primarily of a blue-ice runway covered with a thin layer of compacted snow. With a length of 2,900 metres (9,514 feet) and a width of sixty metres (197 feet), the runway is perfectly suitable for the operation of cargo aircraft like the Il-76. The runway is reconstructed every year after the winter and requires a lot of maintenance to be kept operational, in particular after snow storms that can even occur during the summer months.

Apart from the runway itself, there is a small apron and on a busy day there can easily be three aircraft around at the same time. In addition to that, there is a number of small container buildings and tents and all the facilities necessary to handle cargo, like forklifts and transport vehicles, most of them mounted on skids.

In the summer season, twelve people from ALCI and five runway maintenance specialists are on permanent duty to ensure smooth operations. Some well-heated tents offer accommodation for transit passengers on their way to or from another destination in Antarctica. During the summer months, at least one weekly flight is operated between Cape Town and Novo Airbase.

Weather conditions dictate operations much more than they do anywhere else in the world. All passengers travelling on the Il-76 on say Monday evening (usually the Ilyushin flies overnight) are told to be in Cape Town at least a day ahead of the planned departure. In case weather conditions change (and they do quite frequently), not only can flights be delayed, but also be brought forward by up to a day. Weather conditions have to be perfect for the arrival in Antarctica as the operation is VFR only.

The airbase sits atop a flat area of ice that is several hundred metres thick here. As there are hardly any obstacles around the airport, winds can get very strong and are often crucial when it comes to schedule changes.

The actual Novo Lazarevskaya station is fourteen kilometres (7.5 miles) away, straight downhill and close to the Antarctic coastline. Travelling between the two is only possible by four-wheel drive or a quite unique Russian caterpillar (a refurbished Russian tank).

On some days the runway can get quite busy, as a true hub and spoke system is operated here. Upon the arrival from Cape Town (usually in the early morning hours) most travellers are booked on a connecting flight. Most scientific stations are located up to a few hundred kilometres away, sometimes even further than that.

Connecting flights are typically operated by Basler BT-67s. All of them are operated and maintained by Kenn Borek Air, a company based at Calgary Airport in Alberta, Canada. One is operated in the remarkable red colours of the German Alfred Wegener Institute (C-GAWI, christened Polar 5) and the others operate in the red and blue colours of ALCI Aviation, the company who also manage the operation of the Il-76.

Upon arrival of the Il-76, one or two BT-67s are usually waiting at Novo. They have brought passengers from other stations to Novo Airbase that want to fly back to South Africa and are now waiting for passengers and cargo arriving on the Il-76 to be distributed around this part of Antarctica. On the arrival day of the Il-76, the airbase is a very busy place, full of people from all parts of the world coming and going.

One tent houses a little cafeteria, quite a cosy place, where hot and cold meals are offered throughout the day. Once arrived, the Il-76 can spend up to three days here, waiting for all passengers travelling back to South Africa to arrive. The Russian flight crew spends the time at the airbase or at the guest house in the actual Novo Lazarevskaya station.

My flight to Antarctica is scheduled to depart from Cape Town in the late evening of January 29. However, all passengers are advised to arrive in Cape Town at least one day in advance, as weather conditions can lead to significant schedule changes. Indeed, on the afternoon of January 28, I receive a telephone call asking me to be at the airport at nine in the morning for an eleven-thirty departure, twelve hours ahead of schedule. Weather conditions at Novo Runway are forecast to deteriorate and the schedule is changed to allow a safe landing and departure there.

On the next day, I do as I was told and arrive at Cape Town airport in the morning, where a group of about thirty-five are waiting for the check-in counters to open. Travellers, more than ninety-five percent of them men, are mostly scientists from a number of different countries, including Germany, Belgium, Japan, Norway and others. Although flights are mostly used by scientists going to Antarctica for longer periods, tourists can and do use them for shorter visits.

Minutes later, the check-in counters open and we all receive our boarding passes with seat assignments and can leave our luggage. If I did not know I was travelling to the 'last continent', this would feel like any average flight until now. Even at the immigration counter the inspector does not rise much of an eyebrow when I tell him I am flying to Antarctica.

During the summer months, flights there are rather frequent and it turns out I am much less exotic than I thought I was. Having spent some time in the beautiful departure lounges and some Rand in the duty free shops, our flight is boarding from one of the bus gates in the basement of Cape Town's brand new terminal.

Just opposite the terminal, parked next to a day-stopping British Airways Boeing 747-436, our transport is already being loaded and waiting for passengers: an Il-76 operated by Transaviaexport of Belarus.

Most of my fellow travellers seem very routined, none of them really excited as a bus drives us over to the aircraft on what is a nice and warm summer's day here. Before boarding, all passengers have to identify their luggage and carry it on board themselves. The Il-76 can carry up to eighty passengers but today's flight is not so busy, with only around thirty-five travelling.

In the forward part of the cabin, proper airline seats have been installed in a 3-3 arrangement, like on a Tupolev Tu-154 (and that is probably the aircraft that the seats were taken from). After around fifteen minutes, all passengers have stowed their luggage in the centre section of the aircraft, behind the passenger seats and separated from the rear cargo section by a strong net. In the forward part of the main cabin, a screen and a video projector have been installed and welcome passengers on this service.

A few minutes later, all passengers have settled into their seats, the safety briefing is shown on the screen, everything seems to be meticulously prepared. On both sides of the cabin walls, flags of all the nations running stations or participating in scientific projects in Antarctica have been applied. Outside views are minimal as the Il-76 main deck has only four windows, so the cabin is quite dark although this is now a day flight. The poor view is compensated by a camera installed in the navigator's glass nose which transmits live images into the cabin.

With the main door still open, the engines roar into life, an extremely noisy few minutes but music to the ears of any aircraft enthusiast. With all four engines running, the flight engineer supervising the run-up in front of the aircraft climbs on board and closes the door. We are pushed back from our parking position and are soon on our way to runway 19.

The engines are slowly accelerated to full thrust. This takes a few minutes and we stand on the runway with the parking brake applied. In front of us, a South African Boeing 737-800 is cleared for take-off as we get ready to leave. After just under five minutes, the parking brake is released and our Il-76 accelerates rapidly. The runway is almost on the correct heading so with only a small course change we are on our way to Antarctica.

After around half an hour, some ALCI employees pass through the cabin with sandwiches and also offer hot and cold beverages. For the remainder of the flight, passengers can simply help themselves to beverages, cookies, and more sandwiches that are all stowed in several drawers in the front of the cabin. Sanitary installations on the Il-76 are usually very basic, however ALCI has installed two portable toilets (the big blue ones you see on construction sites or at music festivals) in the rear of the cabin, more spacious and cleaner than most aircraft lavatories.

While most passengers have fallen asleep, today's inflight programme consists of several episodes of the BBC's The Living Planet on the main screen. In between, our flight progress and the remaining flight time is shown.

Anybody who feels like it can also visit the cockpit. The flight crew consists of Russian pilots, navigators and engineers from the Flight Testing Centre of the Civil Aviation State Research Institute. All of them are extremely experienced and familiar with landings on ice runways. The aircraft itself is leased from Belarus and so are the loadmasters and the rest of the flight crew who usually stay in South Africa for the entire summer season. Today's captain is Igor Zakirov, a highly regarded test pilot and Hero Of Russia, as announced on the video screen. Zakirov has operated more than fifty flights to Antarctica without incident.

About an hour before our estimated landing, people begin waking up. On the video screen, an interesting message appears, telling passengers to prepare themselves for arrival in Antarctica and asking them to put on their warm clothes in time for landing. Suddenly, the cabin resembles an anthill with everybody moving back and forth, digging out their bags and changing from t-shirt and shorts into warm winter clothing.

Land is in sight and our descent well under way, easy to follow on the video screen. After just under five and a half hours, the ice runway is in sight, hardly recognisable on the screen as it is basically a white runway on white terrain.

Five hours and twenty-four minutes after take-off, we touch ground in Antarctica. As it is an ice runway, the Il-76 cannot use wheel brakes to slow down, only full reverse thrust. A minute later, we are on our parking stand. Welcome to Antarctica!

Before disembarking, all passengers put on their sunglasses and sunscreen as the sunlight here is intense and the snow reflecting it can cause eye damage or severe sunburn within minutes. Once more, all passengers carry their luggage out of the aircraft themselves, quite tricky when you have to climb down a small and steep ladder with a heavy suitcase.

Next to our aircraft, a Basler BT-67 wearing full blue and red ALCI Aviation titles is getting prepared for its next flight. Passenger seats are being reinstalled. They had been taken out as the aircraft was operating a cargo-only flight coming into Novo Airbase.

Most passengers make their way to the yellow tent housing the cafeteria. Most of them seem to be repeat visitors and not overly interested in exploring the base. You can walk around freely, only the runway itself is off-limits. The weather is perfect today, clear skies with only very few clouds, very little wind and excellent visibility. Wind is actually the biggest hazard to flight operations here.

A short while after our arrival, a second BT-67 arrives. Registered C-GAWI, this is Polar 5 operated by Kenn Borek Air on behalf of the Alfred Wegener Institute, the German polar research centre. The aircraft arrives from Neumayer Station, located around 720 kilometres (389 miles) to the west of Novo runway and will later depart there again, carrying German scientists and equipment.

It is quite remarkable to see how smooth and well-coordinated the operation is here. About three hours after our arrival, the Il-76 has been completely offloaded and refuelled (even the fuel containers are mounted on skids here). The initial plan was to fly back to Cape Town after only three and a half days. However, in the moment we arrived, we are told that the departure would be moved forward quite a bit as weather conditions were supposed to deteriorate significantly in the coming days.

Just over forty hours later, two days earlier than planned, I am back at the Novo airbase for the departure to Cape Town. The weather has changed now, the sky is overcast and up here on the flat ice plateau, it is already extremely windy. The forty hours were the absolute minimum needed to exchange scientists and equipment and, as before, the airbase is extremely busy with arrivals from the surrounding stations ready to fly back home.

After spending around two hours at the airbase cafeteria, well-fed and nicely warmed up, all passengers are taken to the aircraft by snowmobiles carrying a wooden cargo platform on skids behind them. Boarding takes just over thirty minutes. This time, some sixty-two passengers are onboard. The end of the season is near and more passengers depart than arrive. At the beginning of the season, the opposite is the case.

With everybody on board, the engines are started and we soon taxi out to the far end of the runway for our departure back to South Africa. After take-off, the Ilyushin flies some rather steep turns, bidding farewell to the airbase as the captain will not come back this season. Around five hours later, having watched three new episodes of The Living Planet, we start our descent into Cape Town. Once more, a message on the video screen asks passengers to put on their summer clothes, as the temperature in South Africa is a lovely twenty-five degrees Centigrade, around forty degrees warmer than in Antarctica when we left it. After five hours and sixteen minutes, the Ilyushin touches down in Cape Town just after dusk. Three hours after that, aboard a fully-booked KLM Boeing 777 on the way to Amsterdam, it is very hard to believe that only hours ago I was still in Antarctica.

While flights to Antarctica are mostly used by scientists, they are open to tourists as well. While tours are expensive, it is definitely the trip of a lifetime and I would definitely recommend it.

I use a computer programme where I can put in all the flights I take and it gives me all the statistics I want to have: longest flight, shortest flight, number of flights on a particular airline or type. It also draws all my flights on a map, the way you find it in inflight magazines. The line straight down from the southern tip of South Africa is probably one of the coolest things about this trip, when I look back.

Going to Antarctica to me felt a bit surreal. You board an Ilyushin Il-76 in sunny Cape Town and five hours later you land on an ice runway in Antarctica, yet those two places could not be further apart. The most fascinating part of this short visit to Antarctica was really the way there and back. Once I was sitting in the guest house, well-heated and nicely furbished, with food on the table all day and beer and whisky flowing in the evening (well, actually in the morning too), it seemed just very normal. I am sorry to say this, it even got a bit dull after the tenth walk around the area. Not that I want to complain, but this could have been Norway or Iceland. It was amazing how normal life was there and how well everything worked. There was just not a lot to do, so I was happy to go back when the time had come. The excitement came back when boarding the caterpillar for the rugged transfer back to the airfield and to board an Il-76 back to Cape Town. Absolutely breathtaking. Unbelievable!

FlyGeorgia
(intended for Airliner World, announced but never published)

The small nation of Georgia, nestled in the Caucasus mountains, is quite a spectacular and very diverse country and still largely undiscovered by tourists — undeservedly so. Tbilisi is Georgia's capital and the city's airport is the prime gateway to the rest of the country as well as the Caucasus region that is located between Europe and Asia. Georgia's strategic location and the growing interest in the country and the region are what it's newest airline, FlyGeorgia, is trying to capitalise on.

The privately-owned airline took to the skies in August 2012 when its first Airbus A319, registered 4L-FGA, departed from Tbilisi to the coastal city of Batumi. The route between the two cities is the busiest domestic route in Georgia (and one of the few that has the demand to justify flights in what is a very small country after all). Just a few weeks after the airline's entrance into the domestic market, FlyGeorgia's first international routes to Tehran's Imam Khomeini Airport and Amsterdam, both previously unserved from Tbilisi, followed.

A country of just under five million people, Georgia is not a very big market and one already served by numerous airlines. The two dominant ones at the moment are Georgia's national carrier Georgian Airlines, serving ten international and two domestic destinations from Tbilisi, and Turkish Airlines with four daily flights from Tbilisi to Istanbul (and connections to the rest of the world from there). After about a year of operations for FlyGeorgia, one of the conclusions the airline has come to is that relying on O&D ('origin and destination', in other words not connecting onwards) traffic to and from Tbilisi is not sufficient. The solution, according to CEO Bijan Mougouee, is to stimulate connecting traffic.

Tbilisi's airport is a very modern and convenient facility, the current terminal opening as recently as 2007. This, and its strategic location between Europe and Middle Eastern countries like Iran or Iraq and places in Central Asia make it an ideal transit point. Today, the airline is concentrating much more on connecting traffic and its schedules have been adjusted to allow quick connections between flights. This change of plans seems to have done the airline some good — passenger figures are improving steadily and the airline is looking at a number of new destinations, most of them in Europe.

As of August 2013, FlyGeorgia's fleet consists of one Airbus A319 (4L-FGA) and one Airbus A320 (4L-FGC). The airline had a second Airbus A319 (4L-FGB) but this aircraft has been returned since. However, with a number of new route openings imminent, the fleet is soon to grow again. Plans call for a pair of A319s as well as a number of Embraer 190s to join the airline in the coming months. With the Embraers in particular, FlyGeorgia hopes to open a number of thinner routes to neighbouring countries like Armenia (where the national airline Armavia has just gone bankrupt and left a gap in direct flights from the capital Yerevan) and Azerbaijan.

The choice of destinations, in the case of FlyGeorgia, is not necessarily the airline's choice alone. Often, bilateral agreements with other countries restrict the number of airlines that can operate between them, usually down to a single airline from each end of the route; so on flights from Georgia to Israel and Russia (both busy and 'natural' markets from Georgia), FlyGeorgia is not currently able to get permission to operate, as there is already another Georgian carrier flying to them. Following tensions with Russia, flights between both countries had been stopped entirely and passengers had to use transit points like the Ukraine or Turkey to travel between Georgia and Russia.

Additionally, with Georgian Airways owned by the government, the support for a domestic competitor on a route that the national airline is already serving is not always enthusiastic. In the beginning, the relations between Georgian Airways and the new kid in town, FlyGeorgia, was quite reserved. Now, it seems, both airlines have found a more pragmatic approach to things and come to realise that it will be hard enough to deal with competitors like Turkish Airlines or Pegasus and it is a waste of time to fight each other more than necessary. On the lucrative routes from Tbilisi to Iraq, an agreement has now been found with both airlines serving two destinations in Iraq each and thus sharing the market in a way that makes it profitable for both parties — FlyGeorgia operates from Tbilisi to Baghdad and Najaf while Georgian Airways serve Erbil and Suleymaniyah.

This agreement could be extended to other countries in the near future. As Bijan Mougouee of FlyGeorgia notes, the Georgian government has taken a more supportive approach in recent months and maybe realised that a certain degree of competition is not necessarily bad. Georgia was hugely popular as a tourist destination in the era of the Soviet Union — well known for beaches, mountains, great food and wine, and still receives a steady flow of visitors from the countries that were formerly part of the USSR. The number of tourists from the rest of Europe is still rather low at the moment — albeit growing. More tourists visiting Georgia could of course also mean more potential passengers for FlyGeorgia. The airline thus recently teamed up with the Georgian Ministry of Tourism to jointly promote Georgia as a tourist destination and FlyGeorgia's direct flights to Tbilisi from Europe.

Future destinations for FlyGeorgia will include more cities in Europe (flights to Frankfurt, Stockholm and London Luton are about to launch, and plans to serve Barcelona are quite concrete) as well as Delhi in India, a market currently not served from Tbilisi. Bijan Mougouee explains: "With the current fleet of just two aircraft, we can not serve all the destinations we want to serve, we have to be selective. With the arrival of the Embraer 190s, more regional destinations like Yerevan or Baku are likely to follow, which do not support the operation of an Airbus."

Another thing with new routes is that they do not always work the way an airline wants them to. The domestic route to Batumi has been discontinued as have the flights to Amsterdam (the airline launched a route to nearby Dusseldorf in Germany instead, which is developing rather well according to the CEO). Another route that has already been launched is to Brussels, a destination that has not previously seen direct flights.

Flights to Europe usually leave Tbilisi in the morning and arrive back in the early evening. This timetable is very convenient for travellers, as most airlines operating into Tbilisi do so in the middle of the night. Connecting services from Tbilisi to places in Iran, Iraq or Egypt mostly operate at night, allowing connections in both directions. In addition to scheduled flying, FlyGeorgia is also operating charter flights to sunny spots in the Mediterranean and Egypt and also to Kuwait and extra flights to Baghdad. These mostly operate from Tbilisi but also from Batumi.

FlyGeorgia defines itself as a full service airline and on flights to Europe provides quite a good inflight service, with hot meals, a good choice of beverages (including lovely Georgian wine), pillows and blankets, all free of charge. In business class, it offers an enhanced experience, with real business class seats and an upgraded cabin service. A good inflight product, according to Bijan Mougouee, is an absolute necessity when FlyGeorgia wants to compete with airlines like Turkish Airlines, Lufthansa or Alitalia who all serve Tbilisi, or justify higher fares compared to low-cost carriers like Pegasus or Air Baltic.

With the fleet of FlyGeorgia growing, the airline has ambitious plans for the future that involve more than just passenger flying. Possibly with experienced partners, the airline aims to establish both a training academy for flight crews and ground staff as well as a maintenance facility that can also perform heavy checks on their own as well as other airlines' aircraft.

Following the recent change of strategy from relying mostly on O&D traffic towards developing Tbilisi as a small hub and offering connections between Europe and destinations in the Middle East, FlyGeorgia seems to be on the right path. Passenger figures are improving significantly and the airline seems to have made some good choices with its routes. Georgia is a relatively small market and one that is already served by numerous airlines, including the first low cost airlines like Air Baltic or Wizzair (who are flying to Kutaisi instead of Tbilisi but still managing to eat away some market share). If FlyGeorgia continues to build a regional hub, it should stand a fair chance of securing its slice of the pie and route passengers via Tbilisi who are currently travelling on different routings, and stimulate additional traffic.

Competitors like Georgian Airlines or Azerbaijan Airlines from neighbouring Azerbaijan have been rather passive in taking advantage of their home airports' strategic location and to developing into true hubs — and Armavia from Armenia has ceased flying entirely. Hopefully, apart from growing its Tbilisi operation, FlyGeorgia will also manage to attract more visitors to Georgia, one of the most exciting and diverse countries in the region and absolutely deserves a visit.

Some readers of the magazines may have noticed what is sometimes described as 'The Curse of Airliner World'. Airliner World could be replaced by any other magazine title for that matter, it happens to them, too! You read an article about a new airline, see all the nice pictures and learn about their ambitious and exciting plans. A few days later, you are just through with the magazine, this very airline stops flying and goes bust.

Since I have started writing articles, I have always found small airlines and new airlines the most interesting. Given the choice to write a long article about Delta Airlines or Cathay Pacific, or a story about a new start-up in Congo or the Faroe Islands, I would definitely choose the latter. It's just so much more exciting. You have a bunch of very enthusiastic people who have worked damn hard, often enough for years, and more than often invested their own money to get the new airline off the ground — Espen Hennig-Olsen comes to mind, a Norwegian ice cream manufacturer and founder of a small airline called FlyNonstop. FlyNonstop operated a single Embraer 190 and they lasted just about as long as it took me to write my article about them.

Many new airlines don't even take off at all, so it is actually quite a remarkable achievement when an independent airline gets to the point of having an aircraft painted in their colours, all the papers and permits in place and actually operate an inaugural flight. Aviation is probably one of the businesses where it is easiest to lose a lot of money and so much harder to ever actually make some. ("How do you make a small fortune in the airline business?" "Start with a large fortune.") Many new airlines fail — unfortunately — and when as a writer you specialise in new and small carriers from funny places like I do, odds are good that the airline doesn't last very long. My list of fatalities is quite long: FlyNonstop, PLUNA, Air Lituanica, Zambezi Airlines...

One airline that I really liked a lot and that I thought stood a fair chance to make it was FlyGeorgia. And not because their flight attendants' uniforms were the coolest I have ever seen. Georgia has seen many airlines come and go and even the government-owned carrier Georgian Airways doesn't seem to know where it's heading. FlyGeorgia wanted to establish a little hub in Tbilisi, one of the most modern airports in the region and in a good location between Europe and the Middle East and countries like Iran and Iraq, where it served a number of cities.

I travelled to Tbilisi (one of the most wonderful cities I know, by the way) on one of their flights from Dusseldorf, my home airport. In Tbilisi I took photographs on the apron with their entire fleet on the ground at the time. The pictures turned out beautifully. I met the charismatic CEO who told me about the difficulties the company was facing, including allegations that it was a front company for Iranians trying to evade sanctions and invest money in Georgia. He had a different view on the matter. Whether or not these allegations were true remains unclear. My article was ready, pictures were lovely and it was already announced for the next issue of Airliner World when the airline suddenly had to return all of its leased aircraft. It kept on flying sporadically for a few weeks, using aircraft chartered at short notice, before it was shut down. Quite interestingly, their media representative sent me an e-mail a few days after the last flight, when the airline was already grounded and most of their staff probably made redundant, asking when my article about them would appear (I wonder if she was serious?). The Curse of Airliner World hit FlyGeorgia even before the article about them was published.

Churchill Airport, Gateway to the Polar Bear Capital
(appeared in Airports of the World May/June 2010)

The Canadian town of Churchill, located at the shores of Hudson Bay in the province of Manitoba, is a small community with only one thousand people living there year round. Small it may be, but its location makes it an important staging post for anybody heading further north. It is Canada's only significant inland harbour, with tons and tons of high-quality grain shipped overseas from here. The spaghetti on your plate may actually have travelled from Churchill to Italy when it was still wheat grains.

The one thing that Churchill is really famous for is probably its furry inhabitants: polar bears. Churchill calls itself the world's polar bear capital. And indeed, for watching these majestic animals in the wild, the area around Churchill is probably unbeatable. Thousands of visitors come every year from all over the world, and the majority make use of Churchill's airport (YYQ / CYYQ), located just six kilometres (3.7 miles) from the town's small centre.

The airport is definitely oversized due to its history as an airbase. Fort Churchill, as the base was known, was first established in 1942 by the United States Air Force as part of the Crimson Route, a proposed overseas air support route to Europe. Fort Churchill was a thriving military community through the 50s and 60s and then the town had around six times as many inhabitants as today. Fort Churchill was decommissioned in the mid-1960s and most buildings torn down. What was once a huge military complex can now only be seen in pictures. Yet some of the infrastructure, most importantly two runways, has been retained for civilian use. Today, Churchill airport hosts a variety of airlines that frequently serve the airport — two notable tenants are Calm Air and Kivalliq Air, both operating a small hub here.

Calm Air operates Saab 340s and ATR 42s. The first Calm Air flight arrives from the airline's main base at Winnipeg Airport at 10am and then continues on to Arviat, Whale Cove, Rankin Inlet, Chesterfield Inlet and Baker Lake, offering some further connections from there. In the afternoon, the aircraft returns from the small communities further up north and continues back to Winnipeg, sometimes landing in the small town of Gillam en route. In addition to the scheduled passenger flights, Calm Air frequently operates its all-cargo Hawker-Siddeley HS748 to Churchill Airport.

Kivalliq Air operates a very similar scheme of flights, with one aircraft (a Beech 200) based at Churchill, departing daily except Saturdays to a number of small towns in the province of Nunavut (pronounced as in, "I'm having none of it!") and returning back to Churchill in the evening. These flights and the onward connection to Winnipeg are essential links for the small towns in this remote part of the world.

Nolinor Aviation is another frequent visitor to the airport, in particular during the main, short, tourist season that typically runs from October to late November. This is the time when the polar bears from the region congregate around Churchill, waiting for the Hudson Bay to freeze. Once frozen, the bears head onto the ice to hunt, spend most of the winter out there and are a much rarer sight around Churchill for that period. During those busy weeks, Nolinor often operates daily flights from Winnipeg to Churchill on behalf of two local tour operators using both their Convair 580 and Boeing 737-200, depending on demand. The aircraft usually arrive from Winnipeg in the morning and spend the day on the ground in Churchill before bringing tourists back to Winnipeg in the evening.

Due to its location, Churchill is a popular stop for virtually any flight requiring a fuel stop in the region, be it delivery flights, military missions or emergencies. In the past, a number of airlines have used the airport for diversions to treat a sick passenger on board, or in the event of a midair emergency such as an Air France Boeing 777 that landed here because of smoke in the cockpit in 2002. As no stairs for such a large airliner were available at that time, one emergency slide was deployed for crew members to get off and back on the plane, which was then grounded until a new slide could be fitted. In November 2008, a Lufthansa Airbus A340-600 en route from Vancouver to Frankfurt landed in Churchill with a sick passenger on board requiring immediate medical assistance. Those are just two examples of a number of big airliners using Churchill as diversion airport.

Interestingly, were it not for the airport's rather limited fire fighting capabilities (it largely depends on the town's voluntary fire department), even more flights would probably use Churchill as a diversion airport. A study published in 2008 by Transport Canada has shown that upgraded rescue and fire fighting services at Churchill would allow a number of transatlantic flights to use more direct routings, thus saving both time and fuel.

In November 2009, Churchill Airport served as a completely different gateway: the Olympic Torch, headed for Vancouver, where the 2010 Winter Games are taking place, passed through Churchill and flew in and out of Churchill Airport (arriving from Thompson, Manitoba and departing to Alert, Nunavut, the world's northernmost permanent airport) onboard an Air North Boeing 737-200. Because of the extremely low temperatures Churchill often experiences during the winter, Bombardier has chosen the airport in the past to run cold-weather tests with new aircraft during certification, including both the Dash 8-400 propliner and the Challenger bizjet.

The terminal at Churchill Airport is quite small but perfectly adequate for the number of passengers passing through. Only when a Boeing 737 arrives, bringing new tourists visiting to watch the polar bears, does it ever get crowded. The small building has all the basic amenities you would expect from an airport the size of Churchill. Arriving and departing passengers use the same terminal area. All passengers walk between aircraft and terminal (only a few steps, but in minus forty degrees Celsius, even those can get very chilly). Besides a row of check-in counters and a luggage belt, the terminal features a small cafeteria and a vending machine for when the cafeteria is closed. Some memorabilia depicts the history of Churchill and some apparently have been given to the airport as a 'thank you' by airlines that had to divert here. The control tower is located in front of the terminal building, just across the small car park. The terminal does not usually have customs and immigration facilities, as flights operating here are only domestic. However, upon request the provision of customs and immigration can be arranged, as customs officers are usually working in Churchill's port, at least during the summer months.

The airport has two runways, 15/33 (measuring 9,200 feet

or 2,804 metres) and a shorter one, 7/25 (4,000 feet long, equalling 1,219 metres). As the airport is never really busy, the longer of the two handles most flights.

Closer to the town centre, the heliport operated by Hudson Bay Helicopters is used for sightseeing flights as well as fire suppression and mineral exploration. It is not unusual that polar bears that are caught dangerously close to the town are placed back into the wild by helicopter.

During the summer months, a small water aerodrome operates near Churchill. Floatplanes provide flights to lodges in the area of Churchill from here, as no roads connect Churchill to the outside world. During the winter, when everything is frozen, the water aerodrome remains closed.

All in all, Churchill fulfils an important role for the entire region, providing much-needed links to the outside world for locals when there are often no road links between the different communities. Should the facilities at Churchill Airport be upgraded and the airport become a designated diversion airport, traffic (although for rather unpleasant reasons) may well increase. With tourism in Churchill growing, it does not seem unlikely that international airlines will operate the occasional charter here. One German tour operator is apparently planning a direct flight from Europe to Churchill for 2011. For the regular traffic operating here, Churchill Airport offers passengers a pleasant and convenient welcome to the Polar Bear Capital.

Finally, an interesting sight for people interested in aviation is 'Miss Piggy'. She is a Curtiss C-46, or more accurately the leftovers of one, which crashed near Churchill in November 1979. The plane got its nickname because rather frequently, pigs were the cargo on board. 'Miss Piggy' can be found on a scenic small road about halfway between Churchill and the airport, on the shores of Hudson Bay. The plane can even be found as a local attraction on Churchill maps. On the day it crashed, the aircraft was carrying a cargo of soda cans to be flown to Chesterfield Inlet. Suffering an engine problem after take-off, the apparently overloaded aircraft had to return to Churchill. However, it did not make it there but crashed a few kilometres away from the airport on a rocky cliff after hitting some trees and cutting a power line. There were no fatalities and legend has it that at least one of the pilots was found drinking in a local bar in Churchill when rescuers were searching for the crew.

The trip to Churchill was a brief one and had not much to do with the airport. At the time, the company I was part of, Airevents, had operated sightseeing flights to the North Pole, which worked very well and continue to this day. We were looking at new projects and one of them was a direct flight from Germany to Churchill, bringing in tourists for the weekend, visit the polar bears, fly back home, and was obliquely referred to in the article. A Churchill travel agency invited me to join one of their tours as they were keen to work with us. The one and a half days I spent in Churchill were fantastic. It is a very unique town and we would have loved to start those tours. It was little but stubborn obstacles, like insurance matters, no customs at the airport in Churchill during winter, and many other small things which stopped it happening. The article about Churchill Airport is a by-product of my short visit there.

Syrianair

(appeared in Airliner World November 2006)

The history of Syria's flag carrier goes back to 1947. The airline started operations in the summer of 1947 under the name of Syrian Airways, using a small fleet of two Beech 18s and three Douglas DC-3s, all of them acquired second-hand. The network back then was in many ways similar to that of today, covering the domestic destinations of Aleppo, Latakia, Qamishli and Palmyra; and Baghdad, Beirut, Cairo, Jeddah and Kuwait internationally. The operation was based in Damascus — at Mezze airport near the city centre — and backed by Pan American Airways.

However, Syrian Airways did not last for long. After less than a year, the airline had to cease operations due to financial difficulties and the Palestine war. Flights re-started only in 1952, without former partner Pan American. The fleet then consisted of Douglas DC-3s, the Beech 18s having been disposed of. The first years of operations were full of difficulties, with a number of aircraft accidents, the worst being the crash of a DC-3 in Aleppo in February 1956 which remains to this day the airline's worst accident. The fleet was renewed and strengthened with the acquisition of three Douglas DC-4s in 1958, allowing for new destinations to be opened and extra capacity on existing routes.

In 1958, in the cause of Arab unity, Syria and Egypt merged to become a single nation — the United Arab Republic. Consequently, the two flag carriers, Syrian Airways and Misrair (Egypt in Arabic is Misr) were also to become one: United Arab Airlines. At that time, Misrair was the much stronger carrier of the two. In reality, the merger did not really change much except for the name, and the operation out of Damascus continued as before. The route between the two hubs Cairo and Damascus became the busiest with two daily return flights. The marriage of the two countries only lasted until 1961 and with their separation (Syria then becoming the Syrian Arab Republic), the two airlines went their separate ways.

A number of more advanced Douglas DC-6s had just been delivered to Damascus, and three of them remained with the Syrian part of the airline. With a fleet of Douglas DC-3s, DC-4s and DC-6s,

Syrian Arab Airlines launched operations in the same year. Things stabilised and the network grew: Munich and Rome were added, both being served in a combined weekly DC-6 service. Other newer destinations included Jerusalem in Palestine, Nicosia in Cyprus, the Iraqi capital Baghdad, Doha in Qatar and Dhahran in Saudi Arabia. The Jet Age came to Syria in 1965, when two SE210 Super Caravelles were delivered to Damascus.

More European destinations in particular were added, such as Athens, London and Paris. In addition, flights to India were inaugurated, stopping at Sharjah en route, an oddball stopover that lasts right up to the present day. The summer timetable for 1966 shows marvellous routings such as Damascus-Nicosia-Rome-Paris-London and Damascus-Doha-Sharjah-Karachi-Delhi, both flown by the new Caravelles.

By the late 1960s, the Douglas DC-3s and DC-4s were retired. The Caravelles became the backbone of the fleet, with the DC-6s only operating shorter regional and domestic services. In 1967, Syrian Arab Airlines joined IATA and had already become one of the founding members of the Arab Air Carriers Organization (AACO). Time and again, wars disrupted the airline's services: the Six Day War in 1968 spelled the end of flights from Arab capitals to Jerusalem when the city was annexed by Israel; and more disruption in the region followed in 1973 with the Yom Kippur War.

Nevertheless, Syrian Arab Airlines continued its expansion throughout the 1970s, with two further Super Caravelles joining the fleet and new routes opened to Abu Dhabi and Moscow. 1973 saw the opening of the new Damascus airport, southeast of the capital, replacing the airport in Mezze, which was quite limited in space and expansion opportunities.

Throughout the 1970s and 1980s, Syria's links with the Soviet Union and other communist countries were quite close. As a result Moscow became a new destination and was followed by the likes of Berlin (Schonefeld, gateway to the GDR), Budapest and Sofia. Another consequence of Syria's drift into the Soviet sphere was the acquisition of a number of Russian-built aircraft for Syrian Arab Airlines. Most of them were used for transport purposes by the Air Force but were operated by and carrying the markings of Syrian Arab Airlines, such as the Tupolev Tu-154, Antonov An-24 and An-26, Ilyushin Il-76 and Yakovlev Yak-40. It was only the Yak-40s which saw frequent use by the airline, and remain in service today on domestic routes.

By the mid of the 1970s, Syrian Arab Airlines had become a pure jet operator. A range of elderly Boeing 707s were leased from British Airtours and British Midland respectively throughout the 1970s to operate mostly on European routes. Thinner routes to Eastern Europe and regional services were mostly flown by the Caravelles. New additions to the network focussed on North Africa and the Arabian peninsula: Tripoli and Benghazi, Casablanca, Algiers and Tunis were all added and served mostly on combined flights. Sanaa and Tehran became new destinations as well. At the same time, fleet renewal was on the way and the (then) state-of-the-art Boeing 727-200 (three) and Boeing 747SP (two) were ordered from Boeing and delivered soon afterwards.

With the delivery of the new Boeings, Syrian Arab Airlines started calling itself Syrianair for short, a much more practical name for travellers. (Syrian Arab Airlines remains the airline's official name today.) While the Boeing 727s replaced the leased Boeing 707s (and to some extent the Caravelles), the new Boeing 747SPs were used on the routes with the highest loads — London in particular, the Gulf Region and India, still operating on these routes today. Syrianair began bene-fitting strongly from the current stream of travellers between India and the United Kingdom, offering connections on that route and attractive fares. The extreme range of the Boeing 747SP was never really capital-ised on as a planned direct flight to New York — to be jointly operated with Alia of Jordan — never came to fruition. At that time, passenger figures steadily remained at around half a million travellers annually.

In the 1980s, Syrianair's fleet of Boeing 727s and Boeing 747s was quite modern and up to date. However, the relations with the West (and in particular the United States) deteriorated in the early 1980s, caused by Syria's opposing positions regarding conflicts in the region (Iran, Lebanon, Israel). Eventually, an embargo was imposed against Syria by the United States. A result for Syrianair was that they could not purchase any new aircraft from the West. As the country drew closer to the Soviet Union at that time, so did its flag carrier, purchasing six

Tupolev Tu-134s and Tu-154s, all delivered between 1983 and 1986. These new aircraft gave Syrianair the additional capacity to open new routes and secure existing services.

In the late 1980s, passenger figures had dropped significantly from around half a million in the previous years to only around 350,000 in 1988. Tensions between Britain and Syria forced Syrianair to temporarily (until 1991) suspend flights to the British capital, which only added to the difficult situation.

By the early 1990s, things finally started to turn in the airline's favour. This time, Syria was standing on the same side as the West, supporting the US-led coalition in the Gulf War against Iraq (which had invaded Kuwait). The immediate results were the partial lifting of the sanctions, allowing Syrianair to purchase new western-built aircraft, the permission to restart London flights, and a significant (and free) gift from Kuwait: three Boeing 727-200s, formerly owned by Kuwait Airways, were handed to Syrianair.

A replacement for the Boeing 727s however was already appearing on the horizon as Syrianair placed an order for six new Airbus A320s, the first being delivered to Damascus in the new, mainly white, livery in 1998. The delivery of the new aircraft allowed the airline to phase out the ageing Caravelles and Tupolev 134s (except for two) and some of the older Boeing 727s. Some new routes were opened (or reopened), including Tripoli, Vienna, Amman and Baghdad.

Most recently, Syrianair has concentrated on expanding service on profitable routes and reduced or completely closed the ones it was losing money on, in particular on the Arabian peninsula. The latest additions to the network are Barcelona, Benghazi, Copenhagen, Milan and Manchester. In 2005, Syrianair carried more than one million passengers for the first time in its existence and continues to stream-line its schedule. One of the significant differences compared to other airlines is the fact that many of Syrianair services are multiple sector flights. Most flights from Damascus to Europe stop en route in Aleppo and sometimes route via another European destination. As an example, the Berlin flight routes through Aleppo and Vienna, the Manchester flight is combined with London Heathrow, and Barcelona routes through Marseille. Its European network in 2006 still covers an impressive twenty-one destinations, although most of them only see one or two weekly flights.

The most pressing need for Syrianair is the acquisition of new aircraft, replacing the remaining Boeing 727s (the last Boeing 727 flight is to take place in 2008) and the Boeing 747SPs, which are now all close to 30 years old. I spoke to Syrianair's CEO Nuraat Numir and according to him, it is quite likely that four aircraft of the A320 family will be delivered to Syrianair very shortly. Those might (against Syrianair's principles) for the first time be leased aircraft, as otherwise no delivery slots would be available at short notice. Sticking to the A320 family makes sense, as both flight and maintenance crews know the aircraft well and no additional training would be necessary.

For its longhaul needs, Syrianair plans the acquisition of three new aircraft. Numir stresses that while the purchase of Airbuses (A330 or A340-500) is not unlikely here, Syrianair has for a long time been a Boeing customer and a happy one. While two of the three new longhaul aircraft would primarily replace the Boeing 747SPs, the third could be used for an expansion of the airline's network. Syrianair is particularly looking at South America for this. Caracas, Buenos Aires and Sao Paulo all have large Syrian communities and could be possible new destinations. In Asia, demand would be strong for services to Malaysia and Thailand in particular. Currently, Syrianair's strongest routes are to London, Paris and Frankfurt in Europe plus the Persian Gulf and India.

Phoenician Express is a project that has been written about a number of times. The new airline is to be a joint-venture between Syrianair and Middle East Airlines (MEA) of Lebanon. The airline's two bases would be in Beirut and Damascus. In Damascus however, it would not serve the Damascus International Airport but the old Mezze Airport, which is virtually downtown. Mezze is today mostly used by military flights (like visiting heads of state) and not for commercial flights. With facilities there being upgraded it is bound to become a pleasant facility for travellers, allowing short check-in times. Apart from that, it is only ten minutes drive there from the heart of the city. No order has been placed for aircraft so far but according to Numir, the choice is likely to be between the ATR and De Havilland Dash Eight families, and a decision is to be taken by summer 2006. However, as the relations between the two neighbouring countries became extremely tense following the murder of former Lebanese prime minister Hariri, all but proven to be the work of Syria's secret service, this project has been temporarily halted.

In Syrianair's own network, the opening of new routes is not planned for the immediate future. Instead, additional frequencies will be offered on its successful routes to Paris, London and Dubai when the aircraft become available.

Syrianair is one of the founding members of the Arabesk alliance of Arab airlines. The first step of the airlines in working together will be the streamlining of timetables to allow more suitable connections between Muscat and Casablanca, feeding passengers into the respective airlines' hubs. As of now, it remains largely unclear how deep the co-operation between the participating carriers will eventually be. Many of its services are codeshare flights already, for example with KLM, Austrian, Saudia or Gulf Air and this is to be intensified. Additionally, the airline is working hard on the introduction of e-tickets and a more attractive internet appearance, both to be completed by 2007. Not seen by passenger's eyes, the airline has just finished the construction of a state of the art training facility for both its cabin and cockpit crews at Damascus Airport.

Oh what a mess Syria is today and how deeply I fell in love with the country on my many visits there. Damascus, Aleppo, Palmyra, all magic places! Sure, it was a terrible dictatorship and every time I went I had an upset stomach for a week. Yet, my trips to Syria were among the most memorable — Syrians were always extremely hospitable and I was more than happy when the chance arose to pay Syrianair an official visit, a very fine airline by the way and one with very ambitious plans ten years ago. I wonder what all the people of Syrianair I met are doing today? Are they sitting in a refugee camp in Lebanon? Do they fight in the war? Are they dead? Or are they still going to the office in the morning, trying to keep the airline running? What happens in Syria leaves me totally clueless.

Crossing the Strait of Magellan by Cessna 402
(previously unpublished)

Seen from a European point of view, the southern tip of South America is one of the most remote parts of the world. The wide open landscapes of Patagonia and spectacular natural sights like the Torres del Paine National Park make this a region often visited by tourists from all over the world. The biggest city in the region by far is Punta Arenas in Chile. The city's airport is the main gateway to this part of South America, at least on the Chilean side.

For many tourists visiting the area, the island of Tierra del Fuego (which would translate into 'Land of Fire') is the ultimate goal on their travels. The island is divided between Chile and Argentina. The biggest settlement on the Chilean side is Porvenir, a small town of around 5,000 inhabitants. Tierra del Fuego is divided from the mainland by the Strait of Magellan, named after Portuguese sailor Ferdinand Magellan, the first European to navigate the strait in 1520. With the often rough Magellan Strait between them, people of Porvenir do not find it very easy to get to the big city of Punta Arenas by boat. Going by plane is much more convenient than the two-and-a-half hour boat ride and allows easy same day returns. One of the world's southern-most scheduled air routes, it is served by Punta Arenas-based airline Aerovias DAP.

While in the region, a visit to Tierra del Fuego was a must for me and the idea to take the flight on Aerovias DAP had been in the back of my head long before I even got to Punta Arenas. A visit in the airline's head office revealed that the flight is actually very affordable and booking very straightforward. A plan was made to go to Porvenir for a day — travel by boat in the morning and back to Punta Arenas 'the easy way', by plane.

The boat ride was much more comfortable than expected. A well-equipped coffee bar and a school of dolphins which accompanied us kept passengers busy for the two-and-a-half hour crossing. Porvenir itself is a tiny city and offers little in terms of attractions, but the morbid charm of its often ramshackle buildings and the rugged nature around it only add to the feeling of remoteness that creeps over you when you get there. A few hours were easily killed there and with another two hours before the return flight was due to depart, walking the five kilometres to the airport seemed like a feasible option.

Porvenir's little Capitan Fuentes Martinez airport (IATA code: WPR / ICAO code SCFM) is located about three miles (five kilometres) outside the town centre, about an hour's walk or a short taxi drive away. To call this quiet place an airport is an exaggeration really, and the locals rightfully speak of an 'aerodromo'. The road to the airfield is, unlike most of Porvenir, in splendid condition, newly-paved but hardly used at all. The airport terminal itself is another surprise. Its size is very generous, given the maximum of three Cessna 402 flights a day that it has to handle. Inaugurated only in early 2008 by then-Chilean president Michelle Bachelet, it has replaced a much smaller structure which was completely destroyed by a fire in 2007. Not only the terminal but also the airport's runway system also seems a bit oversized: main runway 9/27 measures 8202 x 98 feet (2500 x 29.9 meters) and is crossed by a shorter gravel runway, 3/21, much shorter at 3150 x 98 feet (960.1 x 29.9 meters).

The airport gate guard, a Beechcraft E18S, is the only aircraft permanently based here. Formerly flying as CC-CAK with Transporte Aéreo de Magallanes (TAMA), the aircraft routinely operated on the scheduled route between Porvenir and Punta Arenas. In August 1980, the aircraft suffered a failure of its right engine during its takeoff run from Porvenir, slid off the runway and ended in the grass. Following an evaluation by the authorities and insurers, it was decided to write the aircraft off due to substantial damage to the fuselage and engines. It has been parked here ever since and is now one of very few surviving Beech 18s in Latin America. Although it has been exposed to the often rough climate that Tierra del Fuego enjoys for more than 30 years, the aircraft is still in very good condition. The windows and doors have been sealed and the entire aircraft painted with a coat of protective white colour.

Today, Aerovias DAP is the only airline serving Porvenir on scheduled flights. From Monday to Friday, three daily roundtrips are offered. Due to the unappealing nature of the alternative (by boat), it is quite common, given the limited number of seats, that flights are fully booked. Tickets are subsidised and thus very affordable at approximately US $18 for a single ride.

The route to Porvenir is one of two scheduled services that Aerovias DAP offers. The other route is from Punta Arenas to Puerto Williams, even further south on Navarino Island. Apart from that, the airline operates charter flights to King George Island in Antarctica, using a British Aerospace BAe 146, the biggest aircraft in its fleet.

Its Cessna 402 crews know the route to Porvenir by heart and on my flight from Porvenir to Punta Arenas, the captain predicted the flight time almost exactly right. Depending on winds, the flight time can be anywhere from twelve to twenty-five minutes. For today's evening flight, flight number DAP 15, back to the mainland, only five passengers were booked. Just about fifteen minutes before scheduled departure, a pickup truck arrived at the terminal carrying the station manager, check-in agent, ramp agent and supervisor — all in one person.

As one would imagine, the check-in process was very informal and straightforward. Runway 27 was in use today and the flight from Punta Arenas was arriving from the west, the little Cessna 402 already visible as it flew past the airport on its approach. Deboarding and boarding was as swift as can be and within minutes, we were airborne flying into the mild evening light aboard CC-CLV.

During the flight, which followed a direct GPS heading, great views were on offer as we left Tierra del Fuego and crossed over this arm of the Magellan Strait to the Chilean mainland. Our altitude never exceeded 3,000 feet; when you are used to flying on Airbuses and Boeings, a ride on a little Cessna always takes a few minutes of getting used to and soon becomes a pure joy, even on a windy day.

Just a few minutes into the flight, with most of the Strait of Magellan still ahead, the city of Punta Arenas came into sight to the left. While Punta Arenas' status of southernmost city in the world can be disputed, it surely is the southernmost city in the world with more than 100,000 residents. The airport, Presidente Carlos Ibáñez International, is located eleven miles (eighteen kilometres) north of Punta Arenas, so we actually flew past the city in order to start our VFR approach to one of the airport's three runways. Just a small turn and we were perfectly lined up for the final approach to runway 30. After thirteen minutes (the pilot's guess was fourteen) we touched down gently. Interestingly, the runway markings are all painted in yellow instead of the usual white, an indication of how snowy and icy the weather conditions can be here in the winter.

A very nice little flight experience and an interesting day trip to one of the world's most remote and not really most welcoming places came to an end. Parked at the terminal, all passengers were able to walk over to the terminal building. There, an employee of the airline was already waiting for passengers, offering a most welcome courtesy ride into the city centre.

When in the area, a flight to Porvenir is a very interesting experience. One can easily travel there in the morning and come back in the afternoon and discover the beauty that the town of Porvenir has (not) to offer. For those not limiting themselves to airplanes when it comes to choosing the mode of transport, you might also consider the quite pleasant boat ride from Punta Arenas to Porvenir for one of the two legs.

This article was never published anywhere and I think it's a bit of a shame. The romance of flying in today's modern world of plastic airplanes lies in travelling on little aircraft in very remote areas of the world. And what high level of operational skills and reliability even the smallest operators often reach — Aerolineas DAP are a specialist when it comes to flying around the southern cone of South America and even to Antarctica. The staff in their sales office in Punta Arenas were very rude and unhelpful, but it was a very memorable flight and one I would have liked to share with a wider audience. Having a nice article ready for publication and nobody interested in it is a blow of fate most writers have experienced. Luckily, this is not the case too often.

Lifting the Veil on Iran Air's flight attendants
(appeared in Airways March 2010)

The flight attendants of Iran Air are, as with all other airlines, the calling card of the airline. The full command of safety and security procedures is the prime content of training, as is of course the delivery of friendly and hospitable service in flight. Iran Air's Department of Manpower Development is located right next to Tehran's downtown Mehrabad Airport. Shahrzad Shahraray is the director of the training department and it would be no exaggeration to call her an institution within the airline. She has been flying as a flight attendant and purser for more than thirty years.

When becoming a flight attendant with Iran Air, a high school qualification is a must; a university degree will make the entry easier. The maximum age for ab-initio entrants is twenty-four years for women and twenty-six years for men (because of the latter's two-year military service). When formal requirements are met, candidates are invited for an assessment which includes a test of English skills and general knowledge as well as a job interview assessing the applicant's motivation.Knowledge about the Islamic religion is also tested. A thorough medical check concludes the selection process.

If it's 'thumbs up' for a new applicant, a twelve week training starts (including security and safety procedures, inflight service training as well as ground processes like ticketing). During this training, would-be flight attendants are not trained on a particular aircraft type. The costs of the training have to be covered by the applicants and employment later on is not guaranteed, although training courses are typically only held when demand for new flight attendants exists.

In the past, all trainees have been offered a job with Iran Air once they completed training successfully. The initial aircraft type for new entrants is usually the Fokker 100 and the Boeing 727. Boeing 727 — yes! the elderly 'three-holer' is still alive and kicking in Iran and the country's flag carrier still operates a number of them, all in impeccable condition. Those two aircraft types usually operate on domestic and short regional routes to the shores of the Persian Gulf or Central Asia.

During their career, flight attendants will change to bigger aircraft types like the Airbus A300B2 / B4 and A310, later on to the Airbus A300-600 and last but not least the Boeing 747. With the first Airbus A320 now joining the fleet, this aircraft type will be part of the sequence in the future and probably be one of the earlier aircraft types that cabin crews are trained on.

Flight attendants usually fly a combination of no more than two aircraft types. The A300-600 and the Boeing 747 are the most popular types for crews to fly on, primarily because those two types fly the bulk of international routes where crews have a layover abroad. Although Iranians are highly educated and curious about the world, travelling is still a privilege for most because of the weakness of the Iranian rial (IRR) and because of the difficulty in obtaining visas for other countries; many Iranians have never left the country. It is mostly for all the travel that goes with the job that flight attendants are well respected in Iran. In a group of young people, says Shahrzad Shahraray, the one who is a flight attendant will usually be the 'star'. Also, flight attendants' payment is better than that of office jobs, teachers or similar, with one advantage being that the per diem allowances are paid in foreign currency rather than Iranian rials.

Most flights to Europe are flown back and forth without a layover, sometimes with an enlarged crew as flight times on most routes do not exceed five hours. However, there are layovers in Frankfurt, London and Paris. These are mostly just for twenty-four hours. It can be more when flight frequencies are less than daily, such as on trips to east Asia — crews enjoy three days off in Tokyo, Beijing or Kuala Lumpur. There was even a layover in the Venezuelan capital Caracas for a short while, when Iran Air operated flights from Tehran to Caracas with their Boeing 747SP. In the meantime, Conviasa from Venezuela has taken over the route with their A340 and the layover, just as much as the flight, is a thing of the past for Iran Air.

Asked when and how flight attendants can become pursers, Shahrzad diplomatically replies, "when the time comes for you." It is a decision of the airline, if or when somebody gets promoted to become a purser. Or at least deemed suitable for the position because applicants still have to pass a job interview. In addition to that, a written test has to be passed successfully that includes Emergency Procedures,

English and knowledge of the company. When succeeding, candidates are taken through a fifteen day training course which gets them updated on the aircraft types they will be flying, leadership training is also included.

Becoming a purser was not very popular among flight attendants with Iran Air, as it meant a step backwards for them in a number of ways — goodbye to international flights, at least to longer routes that had a layover, and hello to domestic and short regional flights on both the Fokker 100 and Boeing 727. However, a compromise has been found here: all pursers fly a minimum of one longhaul flight per month. On these flights however, they are temporarily downgraded back to being flight attendants. For the remainder of the month, they fly short haul sectors, where they are on duty as cabin chief. Pursers, just like flight attendants, climb up the ladder from shorthaul flying on the Fokker 100 to becoming a Senior Flight Purser back on the Boeing 747 years later. The 'final level' is not usually reached before they turn fifty.

Speaking of age, there isn't really a maximum age for Iran Air's flight attendants. It is a rule of thumb that flight attendants retire after having flown for thirty years, although depending on demand, the company may ask them to prolong their contract. This was the case for Mrs Shahraray, who is in her thirty-third year flying with Iran Air (which you really cannot tell...). It is very exciting to hear stories from back when she started flying, before the Islamic Revolution, when flight attendants performed some of their training with American Airlines in the US, wore French uniforms and Madame Mondi, French herself, fastidiously checked that flight crews wore their uniforms neatly. Different times...

Standby duties with Iran Air are actually quite comfortable compared to other airlines. In most cases, you spend your standby duty at home (in twenty-four hour shifts, starting and ending at 11pm). In case you are called for a flight, you will be picked up at home by Iran Air's shuttle service. There are also some flight attendants on standby at the airport and those who have driven through Tehran's congested roads know why — getting to and from the airport can take hours. The standby duties at the airport, however, never last longer than a few hours. Sometimes, flight attendants are even assigned standby duty for a particular flight. When the Tokyo flight has left and all flight attendants reported as planned, they can go home. It is a standard practice to hire Tehran residents only as flight crews. Unlike with many other airlines, there are no commuters from other Iranian cities. Bidding for flights is relatively unheard of, although it is possible to bid for one day off per week. Other than that, no flight bidding is possible, you basically fly what pops up in your roster.

Just like in the rest of Iran, religion plays an important role within Iran Air. This starts during the selection, when the familiar and social settings of applicants are checked for conformity with Islamic rules. Just like all women in Iran, Iran Air's female flight attendants wear veils to cover their hair. No alcohol is served on board. That, as Shahrzad Shahraray smirkingly explains, has the positive result that unruly passengers (where alcohol is often involved) are almost completely unheard of onboard Iran Air flights. Religious holidays and weekends are ordinary working days for Iran Air's crews, although a bonus is paid to them.

All in all, around 1,100 flight attendants are currently flying for Iran Air (including five Japanese flight attendants for their language skills, to work the Tokyo flight). Around sixty percent are male, a much higher percentage compared to other carriers; the number of females are rapidly growing however. When visiting a training course, most of the new cabin attendants are female. Immediately after the revolution, only men were hired to become flight crews. This has changed a lot, with many Iranian women working today in a wide range of careers such as politics, business, even fire fighting and flying airliners; as Mrs Shahraray explains, not only are there more female applicants today but they are also more suitable for the job than men — more motivated, better educated, better language skills and other factors.

Since the Islamic Revolution, Iran Air has been affected by the political situation and embargoes. No scheduled flights to the US have been operated since, the only exception being the visits of the Iranian president to the UN General Assembly in New York. Acquiring new aircraft has always been tricky for Iran Air, resulting in a fleet of Boeing 727s, 747-100s or 747SPs that are still active today (and in pristine condition by the way). Newer Airbus A310s, A300-600s and few A320s have been added in past years as well as a growing fleet of Fokker 100s. In spite of the circumstances, Iran Air prides itself in always complying with the highest international standards. That includes cabin crew training, which 100% conform with IOSA requirements.

Working as a flight attendant myself, I started to write a series about the flight attendant colleagues flying for other airlines for the in-house magazine of the airline I fly for. The motivation for this was to make things comparable. We flight attendants like to complain (I guess most people do, it's not just a flight attendant thing) — colleagues flying for other airlines get much more time off, have longer layovers, earn a lot more, get free staff travel etc. I wanted to find out what things were really like and many myths and legends were soon revealed as just that — myths and legends. Nothing is ever perfect, whichever airline you work for. Nobody gets great rosters, free staff travel, a perfect pension scheme without a downside.

And comparing things, seeing if the grass is really greener on the other side, is what these articles were all about. The series continues to this day but in German; the article about Iran Air's flight attendants was one of only two exceptions where an English version was made accessible to a wider audience. Why? Because Iran Air's flight attendants were exceptional in providing true hospitality to their passengers and it just amazed me to see what a great job Iran Air does in keeping its fleet in impeccable condition despite sanctions against the country. There is so much negative publicity about Iran, I just wanted to write a positive piece and tell people that life is indeed very civilised there and there are people working for the airline who just try (and manage to) excel at what they do.

Compagnie Africaine d'Aviation —
a Visit to the Congo's Leading Passenger Airline
(appeared in Airliner World February 2015)

The Democratic Republic of the Congo (not to be confused with its smaller neighbour, the Republic of the Congo), is located in the heart of Africa. Just a tiny bit smaller than Algeria, the DRC is the continent's second largest country. To illustrate its size: you could put France, Spain, Germany, the United Kingdom, Italy and Poland all together and combined, they would not reach the size of the DRC. There would even be room left to squeeze Ireland in! Seventy times the size of its former colonial power Belgium, the country gained independence in 1960. Ever since, despite being an enormously rich nation in theory (there is an abundance of natural resources, be it gold, diamonds, copper or coltan, it is all there), the country has spent most of its existence in bloody conflicts and even today, fighting continues in parts of eastern Congo.

Another interesting figure and one that shows what an important role airlines play in this vast country: Congo only has 1,800 miles (around 2,900 kilometres) of paved roads, most of them in and around the capital Kinshasa and other bigger cities. There are no functioning overland roads and if there were, distances between the country's major cities would still be very long and a car drive unable to compete with a two-hour flight. The distance between Kinshasa and the mining hub Lubumbashi is around 970 miles (1560 kilometres) as the crow flies, and Kinshasa to Goma in the eastern Congo is a similar distance. Flying is the only option if you want to travel between the country's major cities and not spend days in a 4WD on dusty or mud tracks, if these even exist. That is good news for any airline operating in the Congo and excellent news for flyCAA, the oldest existing airline in the country which is currently operating as a monopolist on most domestic routes.

CAA (Compagnie Africaine d'Aviation, or African Aviation Company) was actually never meant to be a passenger airline when it was set up in 1991. The airline more or less stumbled into that role. Brothers David and Daniel Blattner were born and raised in the Congo and have been doing business in the country for decades, owning companies in construction, agriculture, telecommunications and other industries. Running their diverse businesses required them to travel around what was then Zaire (today the DRC) and driving was just as difficult then as it is today. They decided that having their own flying taxi would be the best solution to travel around the country efficiently.

To serve this purpose, CAA was created on February 5, 1991 and started operations with a Gulfstream G-159. It soon became apparent that expanding the airline beyond being a private transport could be another potentially lucrative business.

A number of what would today be considered highly exotic aircraft like the Convair 580, Antonov An-26 and Ilyushin Il-18 operated with the airline over the years on passenger and cargo flights throughout the country. October 2005 saw the delivery of the airline's first jet, an MD-81, later joined by another MD-81 and two MD-82s. For shorter sectors, a first ex-KLM Cityhopper Fokker 50 was acquired, registration 9Q-CBD. This particular aircraft was unfortunately lost in a landing accident at Goma Airport in 2013. The aircraft type, however, proved to be well-suited for CAA's thinner routes and today, the airline operates three Fokker 50s and has recently acquired a fourth from Air Iceland.

Interesting timing: at the same time the first A320 joined the passenger fleet in 2010, the airline also started temporarily operating a DC8-62 on cargo flights. The MD-80s were progressively replaced by more modern and efficient Airbuses and have since been retired. The airline now operates four A320s and expects a fifth from bankrupt Air Australia.

In October 2012, CAA and its main competitor FlyCongo, successor of defunct Hewa Bora Airways, signed an agreement to form a commercial and technical alliance and lay the foundation to form one, strong Congolese carrier. Since then, the FlyCongo brand has disappeared and the CAA brand has survived (although the addition of 'fly' to the CAA brand is a tribute to FlyCongo). By joining forces, both airlines expressed the ambition to be better positioned to compete with Africa's major carriers, have more purchasing power, and benefit from each other's experience.

Today, flyCAA is the country's major passenger airline. Over the years, numerous carriers have come and gone, most of them poorly managed, many of them involved in accidents (and alas flyCAA is no exception here, the airline having suffered several crashes over the years). In recent months, a number of airlines ceased flying, most recently Air Kasai, leaving only the Brussels Airlines affiliate Korongo offering some competition on domestic routes and to Johannesburg, and some smaller operators flying turboprops; the result is to hand flyCAA a virtual monopoly.

René Janata, a Colombian-born German, was recently hired by the Blattner brothers (still the airline's owners today), who knew him from an Airbus event they all attended together, for what he smilingly describes as 'turning a profitable family business into an airline that is run according to international standards. We are now the DRC's leading airline and cover all important routes. Before we expand our business, we want to get our house in order regarding processes, IT and commercial issues, and also improve the product we offer to our passengers dramatically," René explains.

Many of the improvements will happen behind the scenes and not be visible to customers; some, however will. One example: flyCAA's currently three Airbus A320s all come in different cabin designs. On one flight, a Business Class passenger may find proper business class seats, on the next, he will be squeezed into uncomfortable, old Air France seats, with armrests that cannot be lifted up, with just the middle seat kept empty. "We need to standardise our product. Passengers need to know what they can expect."

Another challenge that has already been addressed is on-time performance, which has improved significantly over the last few months. For René, on-time performance is the basis of successfully running an airline. Something that might come in very handy with the airline's restructuring now in full swing is that the airline has always been very cost-aware and not made any losses in recent years and this may be a key factor for success. Ticket fares in the Congo are generally quite high as distances are long and flying is mostly the only option. A roundtrip from Kinshasa to Kisangani, about a one-and-a-half hour flight, can easily set travellers back US $800, depending on when they make their booking. Although online booking is available on flyCAA's website, most customers still come to one of the airline's offices or a travel agency to book their flight.

flyCAA employs a surprisingly international workforce: you can meet Italians or Spaniards among the cockpit crews and being Colombian-born, René Janata was happy to hear that there are six Colombian A320 mechanics working for the airline (just as they were probably happy that they were to get a Colombian boss).

Speaking of maintenance, the airline is currently performing all the smaller maintenance events in its own hangar at N'Djili Airport in Kinshasa. Heavy maintenance on the Fokker 50s is carried out by Ethiopian Airlines in Addis Ababa and on the Airbuses by Egypt Air Technics in Cairo. At the time this article was written, a maintenance agreement with SAA Technical was just being negotiated, the maintenance arm of South African Airways. It is a goal for the future to upgrade the capabilities of flyCAA's own maintenance facility, allowing it to perform all checks on its own aircraft and offer its services to other customers in the region.

As of late 2014, flyCAA's fleet consists of three Airbus 320s (a fourth was in storage in Johannesburg and waiting to be delivered to what will become a South African partner for the airline), three Fokker 50s and a single Boeing 737-200, ZS-EVE, leased from Gryphon Airlines mostly for the route to Johannesburg. FlyCAA is very happy with the Airbuses and the Fokker 50s which are used on shorter and thinner routes. A single Fokker 100, 9Q-CHO, only taken up in 2011, recently left the fleet and has been seen at Maastricht wearing the titles of Ghadames Air, a Libyan operator, and flyCAA's colour scheme.

With competitor FlyCongo effectively part of flyCAA now, that carrier's fleet of MD80s and a single Boeing 767-266ER (9Q-CPD) were inherited. They, however, are not part of the airline's future plans as they are quite inefficient in comparison and the Boeing 767 is due for an expensive C-Check. Like flyCAA's own MD-80s, the former FlyCongo aircraft have all been retired from service.

A major prerequisite for any future aircraft to fly with the airline would be generous baggage capacity, as most Congolese are not in the habit of travelling light. In fact, after the author's flight from Johannesburg via Lubumbashi to Kinshasa with flyCAA, in excess of four hundred pieces of luggage, big and small, appeared on the carousel. "An aircraft like a Canadair Regional Jet would definitely not work for us, simply because of luggage," René explains.

A major obstacle for flyCAA in expanding its business is the country its aircraft are registered in. The Democratic Republic of Congo's 9Q-register is probably the one in the world most likely to be associated with accidents and a lack of authority oversight. All airlines from the DRC have been blacklisted by the European Union. Many companies doing business in the country or institutions like the United Nations, which have a huge number of staff stationed in the Congo, will not allow their employees to travel on 9Q-registered aircraft due to security concerns and / or insurance issues.

Thus, lucrative charter contracts, for example with mining companies, as well as scheduled traffic, are lost to other airlines such as South African charter carriers or Congolese competitor Korongo, which has their aircraft registered in Belgium. "As we plan to expand our business, a quick solution needs to be found," René explains. The pressure on the airline grew when the Congolese government unilaterally revoked the international traffic rights of the country's airlines with Congolese-registered aircraft.

This affected flyCAA's route from Kinshasa and Lubumbashi to Johannesburg. A short-term solution was found by teaming up with Gryphon Airlines and wet-leasing their South African-registered Boeing 737-230 Advanced, ZS-EVE, which has been operating the Johannesburg flights since.

In the longer term, flyCAA plans to set up a South African based company, Trans African Airways, which would operate two Airbus A320s (registered in South Africa) in partnership with flyCAA. This South African solution would help the carrier overcome the disadvantage of being based in the Congo and secure its chunk of the lucrative business with mining companies. In the meantime, the airline is working together with the national authorities and ICAO to bring the country's standards up to an international level.

Whatever vision exists for the airline, much depends on the political development in the country. Throughout the Congo's existence, conflict has always been bubbling and even if things are quiet in Kinshasa, there may be unrest in another part of the country. One of the world's richest countries in theory, Congo could be a thriving nation. In fact, the country's economy has been growing for years now.

If things stay stable, flyCAA has ambitious plans to develop its network not only from its Kinshasa hub but also from the eastern city of Goma, where the airline already operates a small hub for connecting flights around eastern Congo. Goma would be in the perfect location to launch flights to neighbouring countries like Uganda or a convenient stopover point for flights to Dubai from Kinshasa, which an Airbus cannot reach non-stop. Dubai is a very busy route for travellers from the Congo and currently, no direct flights exist. Launching a route there would be an excellent commercial opportunity for flyCAA. The airport in Goma, whose runway was partly covered by lava from the nearby Nyiragongo volcano in 2002, is currently being upgraded by the Blattner brothers' construction company 'Safricas'.

Infrastructure is not only a major issue when it comes to roads (or the lack thereof). The country's airports are also far from being top notch facilities. Except for Kinshasa's N'Djili Airport, none have runway illumination, limiting flights to daylight hours. This hugely limits the airline's aircraft utilisation and makes it all the more remarkable to hear that flyCAA has actually has been to run at a profit for the last years.

For now, the major share of flyCAA's passengers travel on domestic flights, where the airline serves twenty-three destinations and serves every major city; expressed in numbers, of around 400,000 annual customers for flyCAA, around 360,000 travel on domestic flights. Although the airline covers all the major airports in the DR Congo, it plans to seek more co-operation partners for thin routes that even the Fokker 50 is too big for. Some joint flights are now operated by Let-410s of a small Congolese carrier, Air Fast, on the routes from Lubumbashi to Kolwezi and Kamina.

The only international route is a twice-weekly service to Johannesburg, which will soon see a third weekly frequency to make it more competitive. International passenger figures illustrate just how underserved the DRC really is, compared to its population. The entire country counts around one million international passengers per year, a very small number given its population of around seventy-five million inhabitants. This figure also illustrates just how little access to flying most of the Congolese people have. While the DRC is enormously rich in commodities, very few Congolese people actually benefit from this wealth. Most Congolese people can, at least for now, only dream of ever setting foot inside a plane. However, the country's economy has grown steadily in recent years and a wealthy middle class is slowly developing. This, once more, is good news for flyCAA, as demand for flights will continue to grow.

flyCAA is in the most thorough phase of transition in its existence. And, as co-owner David Blattner predicts, one will probably not recognise the airline in one or two years from now. It should be most interesting to follow the developments of flyCAA in the coming months, the leading airline of this interesting country.

The DR Congo was another place I really wanted to visit yet was a bit nervous when it was really happening. When René Janata, a friend I know from an article I did about Rwandair once, was telling me he was now in Kinshasa, it seemed like the perfect occasion to travel there. And being received at the airport, driven around and having everything organised is really the only way I would want to re-visit this country. The atmosphere seemed a bit explosive to me, like something terrible could happen any given time. Good old Schmitz loitering by the pool and here come the soldiers: coup time! History shows us that this fear would not be totally unjustified.

Luckily, no coup happened while I was there and the longer I stayed, the more relaxed I became. The Congolese were super cheerful and friendly. Yet, even the nicest situation sometimes changed within a heartbeat. As my driver and I were enjoying the panorama of the Congo river outside the city, suddenly a guy with a gun stepped out of the bushes, asking for 'assistance' as I was taking a picture. Which, as he explained, was not allowed without official permission. Similar situations occurred many times, usually solved with dollar bills. Summarising my two-day visit in Kinshasa: it was cool to be there, especially in Goma. Sitting in a plane bound for Brussels was even better. Sometimes, I'm a wimp.

To the Caucasus with KMV

(appeared in Airways October 2002)

The adventure of a trip to the Caucasus starts on a Friday morning at Munich Airport in Germany. Between check-in counters of several US carriers, three desks have opened for the departure of KMV flight KV 788 to Mineralnye Vody, or 'Min Vody', as locals call the city — the name a direct translation of 'mineral waters'. The number of KMV check-in desks is not surprising, given the long queues of passengers heading home, their luggage trolleys heavily laden with suitcases, bags and boxes. After a while in the queue I receive my boarding pass and begin eagerly looking forward to my flight one of the most modern Russian jetliners, the Tupolev Tu-204-100. For most westerners, the KMV service from Munich offers a rare opportunity to sample this type.

The aircraft is parked on the high-security Ramp F next to an El Al 747. My first look at the Tupolev from outside forms a positive impression — it certainly appears modern and well maintained. Inside, although still typically Russian in style (orange being the prevalent colour), the Tu-204 is quite different to other Russian airliners. There are modern seats with integral light switches, hooks for hanging jackets and other clothing items, and individual fresh-air nozzles. The aisle is covered with a striped carpet, and economy seat pitch is surprisingly generous in contrast to Boeing 737s and Airbus A320s of some European airlines.

Our aircraft also has a separate business class section for thirty-six passengers in which seats are identical, only the pitch is greater than in economy. During the flight, a warm lunch is served with a good choice of drinks. Cabin crew announcements — at least on the trip to Russia — are trilingual: Russian, English and German. Whilst approaching our destination, a cabin attendant tells passengers about the spa region around Mineralnye Vody, the Caucasus, other places of interest and ways of exploring them. The area is a gateway to the world famous health resorts of Kislovodsk, Zheleznovodsk, Yessentuki, Pyatigorsk and the Teberda and Dombai ski resorts. An abundance of mineral water springs, mild climate and pure air, alpine valleys, mountain rivers and lakes and Europe's highest mountain, Elbrus

(5,642 m / 18,510 ft), combine to attract many tourists to the Caucasus region.

KMV (Kavkazkie Mineralnye Vody) was originally founded as the Aeroflot Mineralnye Vody directorate in 1961. It is alternatively known as 'Kavminvodyavia', which loosely translates as 'Caucasian Mineral Waters Airline'. Nowadays a medium-sized Russian airline, compared with other companies of similar size it is one of the more active and successful carriers. The airline's fleet comprises a mixture of Tupolev Tu-134As, Tu-154s (both B and M variants), and the Tu-204-100s. In March 1998 the first of the Tu-204s joined the fleet, followed by another of the type two years ago. At time of writing, three Tu-154Ms are serving in Iran on a long-term contract with Bon Air.

KMV's employee count is around 8,000, with the majority working at the airline's Mineralnye Vody base. Financially, they seem better off in comparison to other Russian airline staff or public sector employees, because their wages — albeit low by western standards — are paid on time every month. In addition, various social benefits and discounted travel on all the airline's flights are provided for KMV employees.

KMV's route network encompasses a growing number of Russian cities such as Moscow and St Petersburg, Yekaterinburg in the Ural Mountains, the Volga cities of Kazan, Nizhniy Novgorod and Samara, supplemented by destinations in the Russian Far East like Chita and Khabarovsk. Some cities (for example Moscow) are served up to three times daily. Others, like most Siberian destinations, only once a week. Charter flights are offered for tourists from the Caucasus region to sunny locations such as Varna and Bourgas on the Bulgarian shores of the Black Sea, Larnaca in Cyprus, Thessaloniki in northern Greece and to Tel Aviv and Istanbul. Shopping flights are operated to Sharjah in the United Arab Emirates and the Syrian city of Aleppo.

The scheduled route to Munich was inaugurated in 1998. Thanks to excellent connections from Munich to destinations all over the world, KMV passengers can continue their journeys to almost anywhere, including North America. The decision to choose Munich instead of another hub in Germany (say Frankfurt) was an obvious one for Jouri Gordon, KMV's country manager for Germany. Munich covers a wide catchment area and is easily accessible by car or train from southern Germany, Austria, Switzerland and northern Italy. Furthermore, Lufthansa and its partner airlines offer excellent connections to Europe and beyond from Munich. Yet another reason for the move to Munich could be described by the phrase "everything new, everything nice," as Gordon explains. Being a modern airport with relatively short distances to cover between flights, Munich is very attractive for both airlines and passengers.

Jouri Gordon also says that expansion is underway for travel to and from the Caucasus. The schedule to Munich has been doubled from one weekly flight to two during the summer months. There is added convenience for the growing number of business travellers, who are now spared the hassle of flying via Moscow and having to change there between Sheremetyevo and Domodedovo airports. KMV is also considering a plan to extend the Munich flight to Valencia, Spain, but traffic rights have yet to be awarded by Spanish transport authorities. An interline agreement exists with Lufthansa, whereby the German carrier can issue KMV tickets, a practice that greatly benefits travel agents. However, there are no immediate plans to extend this cooperation to a code-share between the two airlines.

The aeronautical transport hub for the Russian Caucasus, Mineralnye Vody Airport (IATA code: MRV / ICAO code: URMM) hosts a large number of airlines. Besides KMV, other regular users are Vnukovo Airlines, serving Moscow daily with an Ilyushin Il-86, Pulkovo, operating to St Petersburg several times a week, and Dalavia with Ilyushin Il-62 flights from Khabarovsk in the southeastern tip of Siberia. Armenian Airlines operates daily to the Armenian capital of Yerevan using Yakovlev Yak-40s, a type also used by Elbrus Avia, named after the highest mountain in the Caucasus, which is based in Nalchik.

Airport timetables may be obtained from places like the railway station, hotels or the city ticket office, but — curiously enough — not at the airport. On these timetables, no airlines are distinguished, with only flight numbers and destinations supplied. Additional flights or changes are annotated by hand — in blue ink for KMV flights, or black for all other airlines. The airport has two terminal buildings: a small one for some arriving flights; and the main terminal for departures and the other arriving flights — a seemingly illogical situation (nobody was able to tell me which arrivals go to which terminal). Non-passengers are allowed into the terminal building only after submitting to inspection of their passports. The building has a typical Soviet look, in this case cement-gray on the outside with dark brown and light blue hues dominating the interior. Inside the terminal a few shops run by Caucasian babushkas (old Russian women) supply travellers with their basic needs.

Mineralnye Vody is an interesting place for aviation enthusiasts. The terminal building has a terrace on its roof, from where all apron and runway movements may be observed. However, photography is strictly forbidden and offenders risk confiscation of their cameras.

On the opposite side of the single runway there is a large maintenance hangar, also run by KMV, with Tu-154s from different airlines parked on the apron, awaiting maintenance or the ignominy of scrapping. This engineering base affords KMV the advantage of carrying out all its maintenance work in-house. In another corner of the airport, around two dozen gray Antonov An-2 biplanes lie decaying, waiting for a mission that will never come.

With planning for construction of a new terminal underway, the future is looking good. Local authorities have recognised the tourism potential of this beautiful mountainous region and are accordingly taking steps to entice more visitors. But much will depend on the outcome of the ethnic conflicts in nearby autonomous republics, the most well known being Chechnya, only 150 miles (240 kilometers) from Mineralnye Vody. Meanwhile, small improvements are already visible at the airport: for instance an attractive duty free shop, which somehow seems out of place in the Soviet surroundings. The coming years will reveal how successfully those modernisation plans have been realised. Maybe then, travellers to Mineralnye Vody will be greeted by the sight of a bright new terminal building and, who knows, maybe even welcoming smiles.

This visit to the Russian Caucasus was one of the most meditative trips I have taken. At the time, I was one of two owners of Airevents, and we were always looking for interesting aircraft to charter for sightseeing flights. These flights catered to aviation enthusiasts who wanted to sample a particular aircraft type or airline and found it super convenient to simply book a sightseeing flight from A to A instead of having to travel to, say Mineralnye Vody, in the Caucasus Mountains just to fly on a Tu-204. The Tu-204 was a rare aircraft type back in 2002 as it is today, and when KMV Airlines launched flights from Mineralnye Vody to Munich, this was our chance to organise a sightseeing flight on a Tu-204 from Germany. We got in touch with the KMV representative in Munich, a quite cosmopolitan Russian called Jouri Gordon, who also worked for a number of other Russian carriers flying there. He liked the idea and we put the flight together. It sold out quickly and we even chartered a Lufthansa Cityline Canadair Jet to provide extra capacity for passengers who were not so keen on the aircraft type but just interested in what turned out to be a spectacular sightseeing flight over the Alps.

After the flight, I suggested I could write an article about the airline and was invited to fly on KMV's weekly service from Munich to Mineralnye Vody. Although it was a famous resort town, in 2002 at least, there was not much going on in Mineralnye Vody and everything was pretty run down. One day was occupied by a visit to the KMV headquarters where I was told that KMV was soon to be one of the world's leading airlines, planning major expansion and fleet upgrades. Stories you often hear and that you have to take with a grain of salt. The remaining six days were rather dull and it was very warm. I went on a bus excursion to Mount Elbrus, did a few hikes around Mineralnye Vody and otherwise sat on the balcony of my beautiful post-Soviet hotel room in the Hotel Intourist and tried to find the meaning of life (I did not succeed).

Later on, when I was back in Germany, Jouri offered me a job as his deputy, managing the ground operations of the Russian airlines he was representing. Although nothing qualified me for the job at all (except that he seemed to like me), I wanted to give it a try. I even went to Munich to look for an apartment before I got cold feet and decided to turn down the job offer (by the way one of several I got when I visited airlines for my articles). What an exciting job it could have been. Maybe. Maybe not. Who knows? It is in my German genes to always be on the safe side and not run any risks. Maybe I should have made an exception back then...?

About the author

In his early late 30s, Sebastian has loved airplanes for as long he can think and even longer. His second word, approximately at the age of five, was Flugzeug, 'aeroplane' in German, or a slight variation thereof, as he saw the aircraft flying over his head on their way to the nearby Dusseldorf Airport. Not knowing really what to do with his life, he stumbled into a service job with one of the biggest and most fantastic airlines of Germany. Still not knowing what he wants to do with his life fifteen years later, he has stayed there ever since and when not serving passengers chicken piccata or tomato juice, he likes to visit airlines and airports around the globe to write about them. He lives a quiet and peaceful life in a small town outside the German city of Cologne and, should this book become a fantastic commercial success, is seriously looking at a second home in Pyongyang.

Credits

A big thank you to all the beautiful, smart and lovely people who helped with the production of this book: first of all the gang at Astral Horizon Press: Steve Finnigan, Bhavna Vader and Ed Richards. I haven't met you personally but I know you are fantastic!

Simon De Rudder did a tremendous job with the editing and design of this book. Thank you very much for your help, Simon!

Credit goes to comrade David Thompson-Rowlands for organising a beautiful tour to North Korea, which has been an inspirational trip for me in many ways! Long live the Juche idea!

Thanks to all the people at Airliner World, Airports of the World, Airways and all the other magazines, most notably Tony Dixon, Craig West, Mark Nicholls, Andy Martin, Enrique Perella and John Wegg who liked and sometimes even published my articles.

My friend Roman Roth came up with the idea for the title of this book. Without him, we might have used something completely generic and boring. Vielen Dank, Roman!

Thanks to all the enthusiastic people working for the airlines that helped me write some of my articles, in particular Bert van der Stege, René Janata and Hans-Dieter Janecke.

Manuel Kliese and Sven Maertens, my friends who still run Airevents today, the sightseeing flight imperium I used to be part of. Without these flights, many of these articles would not have happened.

Thanks to my dear mother. While she hasn't contributed to any of these articles, she has given me the freedom to go to the airport on my own when I was a little boy and many other liberties. And I think it makes her very happy to be mentioned in this book!

And of course, no man can exist without a loving wife (or girlfriend, at least for now) in the background. Thank you for all your love and support and tolerance. I love you, Nikola!